DYING AND RISING WITH CHRIST

DYING AND RISING WITH CHRIST

A STUDY IN PAULINE THEOLOGY

ROBERT C. TANNEHILL

Wipf & Stock
PUBLISHERS
Eugene, Oregon

Wipf and Stock Publishers
199 W 8th Ave, Suite 3
Eugene, OR 97401

Dying and Rising with Christ
A Study in Pauline Theology
By Tannehill, Robert C.
Copyright©1967 Walter De Gruyter GMBH & CO. KG
ISBN 13: 978-1-59752-991-4
ISBN: 1-59752-991-5
Publication date 10/5/2006
Previously published by Walter De Gruyter GMBH & CO. KG, 1967

All rights reserved.

Preface

This study of Paul's theology is a revised version of a dissertation accepted in 1963 by the faculty of the Graduate School of Yale University, New Haven, Connecticut, U.S.A., in fulfillment of requirements for the degree of Doctor of Philosophy. This version omits some sections of the dissertation which are not essential to the main argument, among them a section which sought to show the relevance of gnostic material for understanding certain aspects of Paul's use of the idea of Christ as inclusive *anthropos*. On the other hand, this version brings out more clearly the significance of the topic of this study for an understanding of Paul's theology as a whole.

Although others have helped me in the production of this study, it is appropriate to single out the debt which I owe my teachers. In particular, there are four men who have assisted and encouraged me at one stage or another of my study of the New Testament. They are Prof. Paul Schubert, Prof. Paul Minear, and Prof. Paul Meyer, my teachers at Yale University, and Prof. Ernst Käsemann of the University of Tübingen, with whom it was my privilege to study for a short time. To these four men this study is dedicated, in token of my appreciation and gratitude.

This study was essentially complete in the autumn of 1964.

Delaware, Ohio, U.S.A., November, 1966   Robert Tannehill

Contents

	Page
Introduction	1
Part I. Dying with Christ as the Basis of the New Life	7
1. Romans 6	7
a. The Significance of Paul's Reference to Baptism	7
b. The Two Dominions	14
c. Romans 6 3—6	21
d. Conclusion	39
2. Romans 7 1—6	43
3. Ephesians and Colossians	47
4. Galatians 2 19—20	55
5. Galatians 5 24—25	61
6. Galatians 6 14—15	62
7. II Corinthians 5 14—17	65
8. Conclusion	70
Part II. Dying and Rising with Christ as the Structure of the New Life	74
A. Dying and Rising with Christ in Ethical Action	77
B. Dying and Rising with Christ in Suffering	84
1. II Corinthians 4 7—14	84
2. II Corinthians 1 3—9 and 7 3	90
3. II Corinthians 13 4 and 12 9	98
4. I Thessalonians 1 5—8 and 2 13—16	100
5. Christ's Power of Transformation as Power of Conformation	104
6. Romans 8 17	112
7. Philippians 3 2—11	114
8. Conclusion	123
Part III. Rising with Christ at His Coming	130
1. The Place of Rising with Christ in Paul's Thought	130
2. I Thessalonians 4 14 and 5 10	132
Bibliography	135

Abbreviations

Bauer (A—G)   William F. Arndt and F. Wilbur Gingrich, A Greek-English Lexicon of the New Testament and Other Early Christian Literature, a translation and adaptation of Walter Bauer's Griechisch-Deutsches Wörterbuch, Chicago 1957
Blass-Debrunner Friedrich Blass, Grammatik des neutestamentlichen Griechisch, bearbeitet von Albert Debrunner, 10. Aufl. Göttingen 1959
RGG   Die Religion in Geschichte und Gegenwart, herausgegeben von Kurt Galling, 3. Aufl. Tübingen 1957—1962
ThLZ   Theologische Literaturzeitung
TWNT   Theologisches Wörterbuch zum Neuen Testament, begründet von Gerhard Kittel, Stuttgart 1933
ZNW   Zeitschrift für die Neutestamentliche Wissenschaft
ZThK   Zeitschrift für Theologie und Kirche

Abbreviations of the works of Philo of Alexandria follow the "Abkürzungsverzeichnis" of TWNT.

Introduction

In using the motif of dying and rising with Christ, Paul relates the death and resurrection of Christ much more directly to the existence of the believer than is done in much theological discussion today. If the believer dies and rises with Christ, as Paul claims, Christ's death and resurrection are not merely events which produce benefits for the believer, but also are events in which the believer himself partakes. The believer's new life is based upon his personal participation in these saving events. Furthermore, these events continue to give their stamp to the life of the believer, for he continues to participate in Christ's death and resurrection in his daily life, especially through suffering. This understanding of the significance of Christ's death and resurrection is too often neglected in Christian thought today.

If this situation is to be changed, interpreters of the New Testament must see more clearly than they have the meaning and importance of this pattern of thought for Paul. This is the point at which this study hopes to make a contribution. The task has at least four aspects, and noting them here will make clearer the scope of this study. 1) Detailed consideration must be given to a series of passages from the Pauline letters. Part of the value of this study is simply in contributions to the solution of a variety of problems posed by these passages. 2) Such details, however, are illumined by relating them to a wider context. A comparison of the different passages in which the motif of dying and rising with Christ occurs enables us to clarify the details of the individual passages through an understanding of the whole motif, while the whole motif is illumined from the details of the passages. Such investigation of the motif as a whole rather than one or two passages in isolation leads to results which otherwise are easily overlooked. 3) This, also, is not enough, however. To understand what Paul means by dying and rising with Christ. it is essential to see the relation of this motif to certain other ideas which occur together with it and show a close connection to it in Paul's thought. 4) Finally, it is necessary to investigate the relation of this motif to certain central ideas of Paul's theology and thereby to determine its function in Paul's thought. This effort will show that dying and rising with Christ is not only a motif which might be fruitful for theological discussion today, but also is a key which opens the way to a better understanding of important areas of Paul's thought.

Previous studies of this subject have missed important insights because they neglected one or more of these four aspects of the task. Attention has usually been directed to certain questions related to this motif rather than to the study of the motif itself. For instance, the question of historical background has attracted considerable attention, particularly the question of a relation to the mystery cults of the surrounding world. This question has recently received thorough treatment by GÜNTER WAGNER[1]. He rejects the thesis of the dependence of Rom. 6 1-11 on ideas from a mystery cult. His argument is not entirely convincing, partly because he interprets baptism as dying and rising with Christ in terms of the full complex of Pauline ideas, as if it were a pattern of thought which Paul originated. However, evidence is presented below to show that this interpretation of baptism is pre-Pauline[2]. If this is so, some of WAGNER'S arguments from the particular understanding and setting in which Paul places this interpretation of baptism are illegitimate. The question of the relation of this motif to the mysteries, then, is not yet settled. This study makes no pretense of settling it. This may raise the question of whether it is legitimate to draw conclusions concerning Paul's understanding of dying and rising with Christ without first having answered this question. Paul's language cannot be cut off from the language of his world. If this motif was associated with conceptions from the mystery cults, this undoubtedly influenced Paul's understanding of it in various ways. However, the relation between the question concerning historical background and that concerning Paul's own understanding is not one-sided, as if we could simply understand the historical background first and then interpret Paul. This study will show that a careful look at Paul's use of dying and rising with Christ is necessary in order to pose the question of historical background most fruitfully. This is essential because pre-Pauline material must be separated from specifically Pauline ideas. It is also essential because Paul's understanding of dying and rising with Christ is influenced in significant ways by the connection of this motif with other ideas, particularly that of Christ as inclusive *anthropos*. If the results of historical inquiry are to be fruitful for the understanding of Paul, the historian must be concerned with this idea of Christ as inclusive *anthropos* as well as the motif of dying and rising with Christ, and, in particular, must consider the interrelations of these and other ideas which were part of the interpretation of Christian baptism at the time of Paul. The problem is very complex, indeed, more complex than is generally realized. This study will not solve

---

[1] Das religionsgeschichtliche Problem von Römer 6 1-11, Zürich 1962.
[2] Cf. pp. 7—14.

this problem, but it should help to sharpen the questions which the historian is asking.

Closely related to the question of historical background is that concerning Paul's understanding of baptism. This issue has also received close attention, particularly in connection with the interpretation of Rom. 6. A number of studies in this area are important for our theme, both because of the importance of Rom. 6 and because some of these studies, such as RUDOLF SCHNACKENBURG'S Das Heilsgeschehen bei der Taufe nach dem Apostel Paulus[3], consider dying and rising with Christ to be central to Paul's understanding of baptism. However, any study which focuses exclusively on the question of baptism will not be able to come to a full understanding of what dying and rising with Christ means for Paul. While dying and rising with Christ was connected in the tradition with baptism, it has a broader significance in Paul's thought. Thus, while the question of the relation of this motif to baptism will be of some importance, this study will be distinguished from studies of baptism in Paul by the fact that it will focus on the motif of dying and rising with Christ for its own sake.

There are some significant older studies which do consider this motif for its own sake. ADOLF DEISSMANN was interested in it because he understood it as "passion mysticism," and so as a part of the mystical core of Paul's religion[4]. JOHANNES SCHNEIDER took up DEISSMANN's call for a special study of this area and published it as Die Passionsmystik des Paulus[5]. Besides being very sketchy, SCHNEIDER's work suffers from the influence of DEISSMANN. He recognizes that "es handelt sich in der Passionsmystik zunächst um einen objektiven Sachverhalt; erst in zweiter Linie um ein psychologisches Faktum[6]." However, he continues to speak of mysticism, and focuses his attention on Paul's experiences of suffering, while giving very inadequate treatment of the texts which refer to dying with Christ as a past event, where the objective aspect comes out most sharply. We will see below that the motif of dying and rising with Christ cannot be understood in terms of mysticism. Any such attempt blocks the way to seeing the function of dying and rising with Christ within Paul's eschatology, and so obscures the connection of this motif with the basic themes of Paul's thought[7].

---

[3] München 1950. The revised edition, published in translation as Baptism in the Thought of St. Paul, New York 1964, came into my hands after this study had been completed.

[4] Cf. Paul: A Study in Social and Religious History, 2nd Ed. New York 1957, pp. 181—83.   [5] Leipzig 1929.   [6] p. 69.

[7] Cf. below, pp. 70—71, 123—29. One of the problems of any attempt to understand Paul in terms of "mysticism" is that the term itself is used in a number of

WILHELM TRAUGOTT HAHN, in Das Mitsterben und Mitauferstehen mit Christus bei Paulus[8], gives an interpretation of dying and rising with Christ which reacts strongly against DEISSMANN's. He emphasizes the objectivity, historicity, and uniqueness of the death and resurrection of Christ. Then he asks,

> Wie kann Paulus die reale, persönliche Beteiligung des konkreten Menschen, der aus seinem geschichtlichen Ort nicht zu lösen ist, an einem Geschehen der Vergangenheit annehmen, das ebenfalls seinen festen geschichtlichen Platz hat[9]?

This one question dominates HAHN's whole study. He solves his problem by bringing in KIERKEGAARD's category of "Gleichzeitigkeit" and asserting that "die Zeitkategorie ist im Christusgeschehen aufgehoben[10]."

> Paulus sieht sich durch das "mit Christus" in die Gleichzeitigkeit mit dem Kreuz und der Auferstehung Jesu Christi versetzt, und zwar so, daß er persönlichen realen Anteil an diesem einmaligen Geschehen unter Ausschaltung alles räumlich und zeitlich Trennenden gewinnt[11].

Unfortunately, HAHN never gives serious exegetical study to the texts which refer to dying and rising with Christ, and so never gets far beyond such general theological considerations. HAHN's concern to come to some understanding of dying and rising with Christ which allows the death and resurrection of Christ to remain unique, once-for-all events of the past is a legitimate one, for dying and rising with Christ does not mean for Paul either a subjective *Vergegenwärtigung* of these events or a repetition of what happened to Christ. But we must seek to understand how Paul can nevertheless assert a participation of the believer in Christ's death and resurrection on the basis of Paul's own categories of thought, not from general theological considerations imported from modern times. This means that HAHN's question will also have to be reformulated, for it is a modern conception of the problem.

---

different ways in theological discussion and so tends to obscure rather than illuminate. I understand mysticism as the doctrine that the individual can come into immediate contact with God through subjective experiences which differ essentially from the experiences of ordinary life. I realize that the term is also used in a broader sense, but this definition is relatively clear and specific, while a broader use of the term tends to obscure important distinctions. By this definition Paul may be spoken of as, among other things, a "mystic" (cf. his visions, II Cor. 12 1-4), but he does not have a mystical theology.

[8] Gütersloh 1937.
[9] p. 88.
[10] p. 175.
[11] p. 97.

ALBERT SCHWEITZER emphasizes the importance of eschatology for understanding what he calls Paul's "Mystik," within which he includes dying and rising with Christ[12]. There will be certain points of contact between this study and the work of SCHWEITZER. However, SCHWEITZER gives principal emphasis to the idea of the body of Christ, interpreted from the concept of the predestined solidarity of the elect with the Messiah. He does not give Paul's use of dying and rising with Christ adequate consideration, and so fails to see important aspects of the function which this motif plays in Paul's eschatology. Furthermore, much of SCHWEITZER's argumentation is questionable, and he has greatly oversimplified the historical background of the ideas with which Paul is working. The connection which SCHWEITZER sees between eschatology and dying and rising with Christ must be put on quite a different basis in order to be tenable.

Recently it has become common to refer to the idea of "corporate personality" as the solution to the problem of understanding dying and rising with Christ, as well as other aspects of Paul's thought[13]. This is an advance compared to previous positions. Especially, it has the value of calling attention to the relation of dying and rising with Christ to other concepts which present Christ as an inclusive figure, such as the idea of Christ as last Adam. But "corporate personality" is a phrase which covers up a lot of problems. In particular, it greatly oversimplifies the complex historical background of the variety of ideas to which it is applied. It is at this point that the use of this idea must be criticized[14].

Although he has published no special study of it, RUDOLF BULTMANN uses the idea of dying and rising with Christ in key places to set forth his understanding of the significance of the cross and resurrection for Paul[15]. According to BULTMANN, dying with Christ takes place when man is confronted with the kerygma, acknowledges the question which is addressed to him through this kerygma, and gives up his old self-understanding. The statement which comes in the midst of his important discussion of Christ's death and resurrection as salvation-occurrence in his Theologie des Neuen Testaments is representative.

---

[12] Die Mystik des Apostels Paulus, Tübingen 1930 (English: New York 1931).
[13] Cf., e. g., ERNEST BEST, One Body in Christ, London 1955, pp. 44—64; RUDOLF SCHNACKENBURG, "Todes- und Lebensgemeinschaft mit Christus: Neue Studien zu Röm 6 1-11," Münchener Theologische Zeitschrift 6 (1955), pp. 32—53; GÜNTER WAGNER, Das religionsgeschichtliche Problem, pp. 305—06. [14] Cf. pp. 28—29.
[15] Cf., e. g., Glauben und Verstehen, vol. 1, Tübingen 1958, pp. 207, 211, 288—89; Kerygma und Mythos, vol. 1, Hamburg 1948, pp. 46—47 (English: pp. 36—37); Theologie des Neuen Testaments, 4. Aufl. Tübingen 1961, p. 303 (English: vol. 1, p. 303).

> Das ist die Entscheidungsfrage, vor die der λόγος τοῦ σταυροῦ den Hörer stellt,
> ob er anerkennen will, daß Gott einen Gekreuzigten zum Herrn gemacht hat;
> ob er damit die Forderung anerkennen will, in der Preisgabe seines bisherigen
> Selbstverständnisses das Kreuz zu übernehmen, es zur bestimmenden Macht
> seines Lebens werden zu lassen, sich mit Christus kreuzigen zu lassen...[16].

Dying with Christ in this sense is central to BULTMANN's understanding of the saving significance of the cross. My understanding of Paul has been influenced by BULTMANN, both through appropriation and reaction, more than the few references to his work reveal. It is not to be supposed that this is primarily a study for or against BULTMANN. However, it does have implications for this question, and we will consider these implications in the appropriate place[17].

To determine whether Paul is making use of the motif of dying and rising with Christ it is not sufficient to look for the phrase σὺν Χριστῷ or the use of a verb compounded with συν-. We are not dealing here with the *formula* σὺν Χριστῷ, comparable to ἐν Χριστῷ, as LOHMEYER thought in his influential article[18]. A formula is only present when there is a clear tendency to express an idea by a set phrase. Instead, we find a variety of formulations: with σύν as an independent preposition, with συν- attached to a verb, and with phrases which do not use συν at all. It is better, then, to speak of dying and rising with Christ as a *motif*. It is not a set phrase, but it is a set pattern of thought which has functions in Paul's thought and is used in constructions which show a definite consistency. The motif of dying and rising with Christ may be said to be present when Paul refers to the believers' participation in Christ's death or resurrection by means of a construction which relates two elements which stand in the same contrast to each other as "death" and "life" and are related in thought to these terms[19].

Paul's use of this motif falls into two major groups: the texts which refer to dying with Christ as a decisive, past event, and those which refer to dying with Christ as a present experience, especially in suffering. To these must be added two texts from I Thessalonians, where it is used with special reference to the future resurrection. We must begin our investigation with those passages which refer to dying with Christ as a past event.

---

[16] Theologie, p. 303 (English: vol. 1, p. 303).   [17] Cf. pp. 73—74.
[18] ERNST LOHMEYER, "ΣΥΝ ΧΡΙΣΤΩΙ," Festgabe für Adolf Deissmann, Tübingen 1927, pp. 218—257. On this see further pp. 87—88 below.
[19] Gal. 6 14-15 is somewhat different than other passages because the contrast is carried through in terms of κόσμος-καινὴ κτίσις rather than crucifixion-resurrection. However, the presence of "new creation" means the presence of eschatological life. In other respects Gal. 6 14-15 is closely related with the other passages discussed in Part I.

Part I

Dying with Christ as the Basis of the New Life

In the passages discussed in Part I dying with Christ refers to a decisive, past event. The ensuing new life is both a present experience and an object of hope. Dying and rising with Christ is here related to two dominions or aeons and their rulers, and indicates release from one and transfer to the other. The emphasis is on the newness of Christian existence against certain dangers of falling back into the existence of the old dominion.

1. Romans 6

a. The Significance of Paul's Reference to Baptism

In order to understand the significance of the verses in Rom. 6 which refer to dying and rising with Christ, it is essential that they be interpreted in their setting. This setting is the contrast of two dominions and their lords. The full significance of this setting will only be apparent when we see that closely related ideas occur in all of the passages which refer to dying with Christ as a decisive event in the past.

This setting has not been given sufficient importance in the interpretation of Rom. 6 3-5. One cause of this has been the desire to draw from these verses Paul's doctrine of baptism. This has resulted in the isolation of these verses from their context. The sources for Paul's teaching on baptism consist only of scattered, occasional references made in connection with a particular problem or for purposes of exhortation. Rom. 6 appears to go more deeply into the question of baptism, and some interpreters see here the uniquely Pauline interpretation of baptism[1]. However, we will see that in Rom. 6 also Paul is not primarily concerned to set forth an interpretation of baptism. Failure to recognize this has contributed to mistaken emphases in the interpretation of dying and rising with Christ.

The chapter is a single unit and is dominated by one major concern, that of answering certain objections which might be raised

---
[1] Cf., e. g., RUDOLF SCHNACKENBURG, Das Heilsgeschehen bei der Taufe, p. 106.

against the thesis of justification by grace through faith. On the basis of his assertion in 5 20, Paul formulates in 6 1 a possible objection in the form of a question: "What then shall we say? Should we remain in sin in order that grace might abound?" That this question concerns a central problem in Romans is shown by the fact that the objection on which it is based is already referred to in 3 8, then dropped until Paul has laid the foundation of his argument, then taken up in a fundamental way in chapter 6. The question of 6 1 is repeated in slightly different form in vs. 15. There have been some attempts to discern a distinction between the question in vs. 15 and that in vs. 1, and therewith a progress in the thought which warrants seeing vss. 15ff. as a new section. If this is so, it might be that the first half of the chapter *is* concerned to set forth Paul's interpretation of baptism. But vss. 15ff. do not deal with a different topic than the first half of the chapter. It is not possible, for instance, to say that the first half of the chapter is concerned with the "transfer to the new order of being" through baptism while vss. 15ff. are concerned with the "proper fulfillment of the new life[2]," for this distinction tears apart what Paul holds together. For Paul the transfer to a new "order of being" *means* a new way of life in service to a new master, and this fact is already made clear before vs. 15. The idea of obedience as slaves to one of two masters in vss. 15ff. is simply a further development of the ideas of sin "reigning" or "having dominion" and of the necessity of "presenting" oneself in obedience to God rather than sin which we find in vss. 12-14[3]. To be sure, some new terms are introduced in vss. 15ff., and the ends to which the two slaveries lead are made clear. To that extent there is progress of thought, but this consists only in enriching the basic idea of the two contrasting lordships which is already present in vss. 12-14. Therefore, vs. 15 is more a break in the style than an indication of a new section which deals with a new problem. A basic division of the chapter at vs. 15 can not be supported, for the ethical concern of vss. 15ff. is present in the first half of the chapter also.

A basic division of the chapter at vss. 11 or 12 must be rejected also. It is true that these verses mark a turning point in Paul's argument, for with them Paul begins direct exhortation. However, this exhortation is presented as the inference which is to be drawn from the argument in the preceding part of the chapter (vs. 11- οὕτως; vs. 12- οὖν). This results in the binding together of indicative ("we died with Christ" — vs. 8; we are "no longer slaves

---

[2] HEINRICH SCHLIER, "Die Taufe nach dem 6. Kapitel des Römerbriefes," Die Zeit der Kirche, Freiburg 1956, p. 52. ERNST FUCHS, Die Freiheit des Glaubens, München 1949, p. 41, expresses a similar idea.

[3] Cp. especially the exhortation in vs. 13 with those in vss. 16 and 19.

to sin" — vs. 6) and imperative ("reckon yourselves to be dead to sin" — vs. 11; "do not let sin reign" — vs. 12), a connection which is characteristic of Paul[4] and which is basic to his argument here. For Paul the imperatives which begin at vs. 11 can no more be separated from the indicatives which precede than conclusion can be separated from premise, and so the chapter can not be divided at vss. 11 or 12 without playing havoc with Paul's argument. Furthermore, the basic idea of subjection to a master which is developed in vss. 12ff. is already referred to in vs. 6. The assertion there that the believer is no longer a slave to sin because he has been crucified with Christ is Paul's major concern even in the first part of the chapter. This is shown by vss. 1-2. It is also clear from the way in which the argument develops in vss. 5-10. GÜNTHER BORNKAMM has pointed out that there is an interesting parallel between vss. 5-7 and 8-10[5]. Both vss. 5 and 8 move from a conditional protasis with εἰ and indicative, asserting participation in the death of Christ as a condition which is fulfilled, to the conclusion of future participation in the resurrection of Christ. This is supported in vss. 6 and 9 by a closer explanation of what this means, in each case connected to the preceding by a causal participle which is to be translated "since we know . . ." (vs. 6 — γινώσκοντες, vs. 9 — εἰδότες). The explanation given is in terms of release from the power of sin (vs. 6) or of death (vs. 9). Vss. 7 and 10 then add further support for these assertions in short sentences connected to the preceding by γάρ, in both cases referring to release from sin and its claims. The major difference between vss. 5-7 and 8-10 is that vss. 6-7 focus on the *believers'* release from the old dominion while vss. 9-10 speak of *Christ's* death to sin and new life to God. Yet these are not two separate things, for it is the assertion of vss. 5 and 8 that the believers' death is involved in that of Christ. The way in which the basic statements in vss. 5 and 8 are developed in vss. 6-7 and 9-10 makes Paul's central concern clear. He is interested in the idea of dying and rising with Christ because it implies death to the old dominion of sin and new life to God. This is the point which is important for his argument in this chapter, and the means by which he answers the question of vs. 1. Only vss. 3-4 refer to baptism, and even these verses reveal Paul's concern to interpret the Christian's present relation to sin (cf. vs. 4b — "in order that . . . we might walk in newness of life"). There is no "baptismal section" which can be isolated from the rest of the chapter because it shows an independent interest in a doctrine

---

[4] Cf. I Cor. 5 7; Gal. 5 25.

[5] "Taufe und neues Leben bei Paulus," Das Ende des Gesetzes: Paulusstudien, München 1952, pp. 38—39.

of baptism. From the beginning to the end of the chapter Paul is concerned with the Christian's relation to the dominion of sin. Therefore, we must ask this question: What is the function of the reference to baptism in vss. 3-4 within Paul's basic argument? Why is it that Paul refers to baptism here when baptism as such is not the problem with which he is concerned?

We do not find the most primitive use of dying and rising with Christ as a baptismal motif in Rom. 6. In Rom. 6 Paul speaks of dying with Christ as a past event, but of rising with Christ as future. In Col. 2 11-13 we again find the motif of dying and rising with Christ used in a passage which explicitly refers to baptism. There, however, rising with Christ is spoken of in the past tense. That we find the more primitive form of this baptismal motif in Col. 2 rather than Rom. 6 is shown by the fact that Paul presupposes this past resurrection with Christ even though he chooses to speak of rising with Christ as still future. This is clear from the parallel between Christ's resurrection and the believers' walking in newness of life in vs. 4, and from the phrases ζῶντας δὲ τῷ θεῷ and ἐκ νεκρῶν ζῶντας in vss. 11 and 13. Paul appears to be modifying an idea which already had a fixed form rather than creating a new idea. The baptismal motif which Paul uses in Rom. 6 already had a history behind it.

The importance of this is often obscured by interpreting the future verbs in vss. 5 and 8 as "logical" futures rather than real references to future time. The argument for this is based mainly on the assertion that a present participation in new life is presupposed and a reference to the future resurrection would be out of place. JOHANNES SCHNEIDER, for instance, points to the reference to walking in newness of life in vs. 4 and then argues that, since vs. 5 is meant to support this, the future verb can not refer to future time[6]. This argument can not be accepted. There is no reason why Paul *had* to use a future verb in vs. 5b if he were not really referring to the future. Ἐσμέν would have expressed a logical conclusion as well as ἐσόμεθα. Furthermore, in vs. 8 Paul makes quite clear that this is a real reference to the future by the addition of πιστεύομεν. This shows that life with Christ is an object of faith, not of sight. The sentence continues by referring to Christ's release from the dominion of *death* through his resurrection. This is something which the believers have not yet experienced[7]. The parallel between vss. 5 and 8 would indicate that vs. 5b is also a real reference to the future[8].

---

[6] Die Taufe im Neuen Testament, Stuttgart 1952, p. 47. Similarly ERNST KÜHL, Der Brief des Paulus an die Römer, Leipzig 1913, pp. 204—05, and SCHLIER, Zeit der Kirche, p. 48.

[7] Cf. Rom. 8 10-11, 18-25.

[8] Cf. p. 9.

It is not true that a real future makes no sense in the context. Paul's thought here is more complex than SCHNEIDER realizes. This is shown by three considerations. First, the dominion of death is very closely related to the dominion of sin, and 5 21 and 6 9 show that the thought of death's lordship, to which the Christian is still subject, is not far from Paul's mind. Second, it is no great step for Paul to move from a reference to present participation in newness of life to a reference to the future resurrection, as he does in vss. 4-5. For Paul these are two aspects of the Christian's participation in eschatological life, and he can easily move from the one to the other, as he does in II Cor. 4 10-14 and Phil. 3 10-11. Third, there is, nevertheless, a good reason why there is no reference in the Pauline homologoumena to rising with Christ as a past, accomplished fact. SCHNEIDER asserts that walking in newness of life presupposes that the believer has already risen from the grave. So it does, and yet Paul chooses to speak of participation in Christ's new life only as something which is now in progress as part of a life open to the attacks of the powers of the old dominion, or as something which is still future. We must now investigate Paul's reason for speaking in this way.

I Cor. 10 1-13 shows that Paul had occasion to oppose a view of the sacraments which regarded them as a guarantee of salvation. Against this view Paul warns of the judgment which awaits the evildoer, and points out that it has fallen even on those who were baptized and partook of spiritual food. "Let him who thinks that he stands take care lest he fall" (vs. 12). It was not only in connection with the sacraments that Paul found it necessary to caution the believers in light of the future. Paul was involved in a wide-ranging battle on this point. An important part of the battle against his opponents in Corinth was waged over the question of whether this sober caution was necessary or whether salvation was already given in the present in such a way that one had nothing left to do but glory in it. Thus Paul exclaims in I Cor. 4 8, "Already you have been satiated! Already you have become rich! Without us you have begun to reign!" — and goes on to contrast the apostle's life of suffering and dishonor to this false fulfillment. Paul also deals with his suffering as an apostle in II Corinthians, interpreting it there in terms of dying and rising with Christ. Through his suffering Paul continues to participate in Christ's death, and this is a check against any "boasting."[9] This caution against boasting in what one already possesses contrasts sharply with the attitude of the opponents, who are "puffed

---

[9] Cp. I Cor. 4 5-18 with II Cor. 1 5-9, 4 7ff., 12 7-10, Gal. 6 14, and Phil. 3 7ff. as they are interpreted in this study, and see especially pp. 88—90.

up" because of their "knowledge" and spiritual gifts[10]. Since this caution is expressed by means of the motif of dying and rising with Christ, which is used to emphasize that Paul *still* participates in Christ's death and so must look to the future for a resurrection with Christ beyond what he knows now, it is not surprising that Paul avoids referring to rising with Christ as a past, completed fact in Rom. 6. The believer participates in the new life in the present, but Paul is careful to make clear that it does not become the believer's possession. It is realized through a continual surrender of one's present activity to God, a *walking* in newness of life, and at the same time it remains God's gift for the future. Both of these aspects make clear that the new life remains in God's control, and the future verbs in Rom. 6 5 and 6 8 play their part in bringing this out. Thus, the tense of these verbs is important to Paul, and they are not to be dismissed as "logical" futures.

The recognition that Paul, in avoiding reference to a past resurrection with Christ, is modifying an idea which already had a fixed form points us toward an answer to the question posed above. Why does Paul refer to baptism in Rom. 6 when he is not concerned with baptism as such? This reference to baptism must have contributed to the development of the basic ideas with which Paul wished to work. For this to be the case, the theme of dying with Christ must have been already connected with baptism, so that taking up this theme brought with it the reference to baptism. It is likely that the connection of this theme with baptism was present not only in Paul's mind, but much more widely in the tradition of the early church. The reference to baptism furthers Paul's argument only if the connection of dying with Christ and baptism is one which is generally accepted. Elsewhere Paul introduces a reference to baptism in order to support his argument (cf. I Cor. 12 13, Gal. 3 27). It is likely that Paul refers to baptism in Rom. 6 because he believes the idea of dying with Christ in baptism is known and accepted by the Roman Christians, so that through it they can be led to understand Paul's conception of the relation of the believer to sin.

This is supported by the form of Paul's argument. The significance of the phrase "do you not know" in vs. 3 has been much discussed. HANS LIETZMANN asserts that ἢ ἀγνοεῖτε and ἢ οὐκ οἴδατε refer "stets auf bereits Bekanntes" and uses this as one argument that dying and rising with Christ in baptism was "Gemeindeglaube."[11]

---

[10] It is striking that the word φυσιόω occurs six times in I Cor., but only once in the rest of the New Testament. The noun occurs at II Cor. 12 20. For further discussion of the "Heilsgewißheit" of Paul's opponents in Corinth see WALTER SCHMITHALS, Die Gnosis in Korinth, Göttingen 1956, especially pp. 145—158.

[11] An die Römer, 4. Aufl. Tübingen 1933, p. 67.

1. Romans 6 a. Paul's Reference to Baptism

This is questioned by OTTO KUSS, who argues for the possibility that Paul is simply speaking in terms of a "polite pedagogy" and is really transmitting new ideas[12]. It might also be possible to limit the reference of ἢ ἀγνοεῖτε to vs. 3, and so see the interpretation of baptism as dying with Christ in the following verses as specifically Pauline. This is the view of SCHNACKENBURG[13]. Both KUSS and SCHNACKENBURG fail to see the subordinate place of the reference to baptism in Rom. 6[13a]. They also fail to see that ἢ ἀγνοεῖτε is not an isolated phrase, but is picked up later by phrases which are related in function and which refer clearly to dying with Christ. In these phrases dying with Christ (in vs. 9, Christ's resurrection) is set forth as the basis from which a conclusion is drawn. Thus, in vs. 5 we find a conditional sentence with εἰ and indicative in the protasis. As BLASS-DEBRUNNER point out, conditional sentences with εἰ and indicative are used in the New Testament, with very few exceptions, to indicate a condition which is regarded as fulfilled, either by the speaker or someone else, and often the εἰ is very close to the meaning "since."[14] This is the case here. Paul uses the conditional sentence as a method of arguing from the accepted fact of having been united with the form of his death to a similar participation in his resurrection. Here the conditional protasis has the same function as ἢ ἀγνοεῖτε in vs. 3, for it also refers to what Paul believes can be taken as an accepted fact and so as a basis for argument. It is significant that Paul has not directly supported this assertion in the preceding verses. Evidently Paul expects his readers to know that they have been united with the form of Christ's death if they know that they have been baptized into his death. Vs. 6 is similar. The argument starts from the fact of the crucifixion of the old man with Christ, this premise being introduced by τοῦτο γινώσκοντες, ὅτι ... The argumentative context shows that this is an adverbial participle of cause. It, therefore, should be translated, "*Since* we know this, that our old man was crucified with (Christ) ..." Τοῦτο γινώσκοντες has the same function as ἢ ἀγνοεῖτε in vs. 3, but now it is clearly crucifixion with Christ which is the premise from which the argument starts. The

---

[12] Der Römerbrief, Regensburg 1957, 1959, p. 297.
[13] Heilsgeschehen, pp. 29—30. Similarly WAGNER, Das religionsgeschichtliche Problem, pp. 292—93. WAGNER points to the οὖν at the beginning of vs. 4 as an indication that Paul begins there to add his own interpretation. However, there is no shift in basic idea from vs. 3 to vs. 4. Rather, the συνετάφημεν is an emphatic way of expressing what is already implied in vs. 3. Cf. pp. 22—24, 34.
[13a] In the revised edition of his work, SCHNACKENBURG recognizes that Rom. 6 1-14 "is motivated by an ethical-parenetic point of view," but still holds that in vss. 4-6 Paul "manifestly offers his own views." Cf. Baptism, pp. 32, 136, 143.
[14] Section 372.

crucifixion of "our old man" with Christ is also presented as something known by and acceptable to the reader although this idea has not previously been mentioned[15]. In vss. 8-9 we have exactly the same pattern of argument as in vss. 5-6: first a conditional sentence with εἰ and indicative, and then, attached to it, a causal participle (εἰδότες). The latter refers to a corollary of Christ's resurrection; the former to an idea which is equally certain to be accepted by the reader: the believer's death with Christ. The basic pattern of argument in vss. 3-10 is clear. The conclusion which Paul wishes to assert is that believers are no longer slaves to sin (vs. 6), and that they may and must "walk in newness of life" (vs. 4), a present participation in life which is connected with the full participation at the future resurrection (vss. 5, 8-9). It is this conclusion which answers the questions posed in vss. 1 and 15. To reach this conclusion Paul argues from an idea which he believes his readers will know and accept from their acquaintance with baptism, the idea that the Christian has already died with Christ. We have seen that ἢ ἀγνοεῖτε in vs. 3 cannot be merely a means of polite pedagogy, for Paul is not concerned here to supply new information about baptism but to argue against certain false conclusions from his doctrine of justification by grace. It cannot refer only to a general connection between baptism and the death of Christ, for in the following verses Paul uses the believer's death with Christ as the premise from which he can argue. We must conclude, then, that Paul is using in this chapter an interpretation of Christian baptism which is known beyond his own churches[16].

b. The Two Dominions

In order to understand what Paul means by dying and rising with Christ, we must investigate the related idea of the two dominions. The contrast between two dominions and their lords is not only basic to the whole of Rom. 6, but is also a feature of all of the pas-

---

[15] It will be shown on pp. 52—54 that the ideas of "old" and "new man" also belong to baptismal tradition.
[16] Mark 10 38-39, in language which probably stems from the early church but is independent of Paul, brings out a connection between baptism and death and between Jesus' death and the death (or suffering?) of his disciples. This is not equivalent to dying with Christ in baptism, but it is close. On this passage see PER LUNDBERG, La typologie baptismale dans l'ancienne église, Uppsala 1942, pp. 223—24. OTTO KUSS, "Zur Frage einer vorpaulinischen Todestaufe," Münchener Theologische Zeitschrift 4 (1953), pp. 1—17, attempts to refute LUNDBERG'S position.

sages which speak of dying with Christ as a past event. It is only by bringing out the full significance of this fact that we can understand the meaning of the motif of dying and rising with Christ for Paul.

The term "two dominions" is chosen because Paul sees man's situation as characterized by two sets of powers which "reign" or "have dominion over" men. However, we can also speak here of two "aeons." The term "aeon" is less true to the terminology of the passages discussed in this study, but it has the advantage of making clear the eschatological setting of this pattern of thought. Paul uses eschatological patterns of thought not only to refer to what is to take place in the future, but also to speak of what has taken place through Christ. The old world is characterized by the reign of certain demonic powers. But something has already happened to change this. Men have already been freed from these powers and placed under a new Lord. Paul understands this change in eschatological terms. It is a change from the old world to the new world, from the old aeon to the new aeon[17]. It is to this change that Paul refers when he speaks of dying with Christ as a past event. The eschatological associations of dying with Christ are especially clear in Gal. 6 14 and II Cor. 5 14-17. These passages will be considered in their proper place, but it is important to have this point in mind if we are to understand the full significance of the two dominions referred to in Rom. 6.

We must now take a closer look at the variety of ways in which Paul develops his thoughts concerning the two dominions in Rom. 6. The pattern of thought which is used most extensively is that of subjection to a lord. In vs. 6 Paul speaks of serving sin as a slave. From that point on the idea of subjection to a lord dominates the chapter, appearing in various forms. In vs. 9 it is stated that death is no longer lord over Christ (κυριεύει). The complementary relation of κύριος and δοῦλος shows the connection of this thought with vs. 6. The same term reoccurs in vs. 14 with sin as the lord. In vs. 12 the image is varied to the extent that sin is thought of as ruling as king (βασιλευέτω). To this corresponds a relation of obedience (vs. 12), and in vss. 16-17 this becomes specifically the obedience of slaves. In vs. 13 there is again a slight variation, for here Paul seems to be thinking of two warlords who receive the service of their soldiers. The term ὅπλα can, of course, mean simply "tools" as well as specifically "weapons," but the latter translation is preferable in the

---

[17] Gal. 4 3-5 brings out these eschatological associations. Note the cosmic background of the thought, the law being associated with the "elemental powers of the world," and the use of the eschatological phrase "the fullness of time." This same eschatological release from the law is the subject of Rom. 7 4 and Gal. 2 19, where Paul uses the motif of dying and rising with Christ.

other passages in which the term occurs in Paul's letters[18], and so is to be preferred here also. Related imagery occurs in vs. 23. Ὀψώνια are first of all the rations or wages of a soldier, though the word could be applied to compensation for other services, and χάρισμα, in contrast, may refer to the special grant which a new lord sometimes made to his soldiers after coming to power[19]. In vs. 13 the soldiers "present themselves," i. e., place themselves at the lord's disposal. The same idea is applied to the slave in vss. 16 and 19. Vss. 14b and 15 are related in that being "under" law or grace also implies subjection. From vs. 16 on, the image of slavery dominates the argument to the end of the chapter. In emphasizing this Paul is developing one version of the relationship indicated by all the images mentioned in this paragraph. This is especially apparent when vss. 13 and 19 are compared, for what is said in the one with reference to service as a soldier is said in the other with reference to service as a slave.

From vs. 10 on, the argument is structured in almost monotonous fashion through the parallel contrast of two lords. Of all the verses from 10 to 23, only vs. 12, which is simply the first clause of vs. 13, and vs. 21 do not show this parallel contrast. There is some variation in the names of the opposing masters. On the positive side we find grace (vss. 14-15), obedience (vs. 16), righteousness (vss. 18-20), and, especially, God (vss. 10-13 and 22-23). The references to God as ruling Lord begin and end the section which puts the two lords in contrast, and it is basically God to whom one is enslaved when enslaved to grace, obedience, and righteousness.

The description of the other lord is much more constant. Throughout the chapter, with only a few exceptions, it is sin. In vss. 16-20 sin is opposed to obedience and righteousness. There the fact that it is transgression of God's law, disobedience of God, comes into play. But even there the importance of the idea of *slavery* to sin shows that something more is in Paul's mind. This other aspect comes out especially clearly in vss. 10-14 and 22-23, in which sin is opposed to *God*. Here it is clear that sin is not merely a series of separate acts nor an abstract principle, but a demonic power, a world ruler who claims the obedience of men just as God does. This is also clear from the activities ascribed to sin throughout Rom. 5 12 to 8 3. It reigns or exercises lordship (5 21; 6 12, 14), and men are its slaves (6 6, 6 16ff.). It dwells within men and there is active, i. e., it works, produces (κατεργάζομαι — 7 17, 20). It has its own law (7 23—8 2). The cosmic scope of its power is brought out by the fact that all

---

[18] II Cor. 10 4 — ὅπλα τῆς στρατείας; II Cor. 6 7 — translate "weapons of righteousness for offense and defense;" Rom. 13 12 — cp. Eph. 6 11.
[19] Cf. Otto Michel, Der Brief an die Römer, 12. Aufl. Göttingen 1963, p. 163.

men are under sin (3 9), and by the fact that it is spoken of as entering the world (5 12), where it and death then reign (5 14, 17, 21).

The change which takes place when men are freed from their slavery to sin involves a change of masters. Now men are enslaved to God. The new dominion corresponds to the old in that it is ruled by a lord who has power over his slaves. Vs. 19a probably indicates a certain uneasiness in Paul's mind about referring to the new aeon as slavery. Elsewhere Paul brings out the difference between the old slavery and the new situation of the Christian by speaking of the latter as adoption to sonship (Rom. 8 15, Gal. 4 3-5), or as freedom (II Cor. 3 17; Gal. 5 1, 13). However, he also speaks elsewhere of "belonging to Christ" (I Cor. 15 23; Gal. 3 29, 5 24), and of being "slave of Christ" (Rom. 1 1, I Cor. 7 22, Gal. 1 10, Phil. 1 1, cf. also I Cor. 6 20 and 7 23). Furthermore, he does not give up the image of slavery at Rom. 6 19. Indeed, it is essential to his argument in this chapter. It is a key part of the theological basis of Paul's ethics[20]. The Christian cannot lead a life of sin while under grace just because the new master, like the old, has a complete claim to his service and holds him in his power. In the new aeon as well as the old he stands under a master who commands him and acts through him. Paul adds vs. 19a not because the idea of slavery is false, but because it does not cover all that Paul would wish to say. It is not easy to explain what is both slavery and freedom at the same time.

The idea that man's existence is characterized by the rule of certain powers has parallels in the world of which Paul was a part. KARL GEORG KUHN has pointed out that there is a connection between Rom. 6 and the section of the "Manual of Discipline" of the Qumran Community which has been entitled "The Two Spirits in Man" (iii, 13—iv, 26)[21]. There we find a dualism of two spirits who exercise dominion over their respective "sons." The dominion of the one spirit is expressed through evil acts on the part of men, and will lead to eternal perdition. The dominion of the other spirit is expressed through good acts on the part of men, and will lead to eternal blessedness. We find these same conceptions in Rom. 6. Related ideas are also found in "The Testaments of the Twelve Patriarchs," where Beliar is spoken of as one who can "have dominion over" men[22]. Paul also takes up ideas from an anti-cosmic dualism,

---

[20] Cf. pp. 81—82.
[21] "New Light on Temptation, Sin, and Flesh in the New Testament," The Scrolls and the New Testament, ed. Krister Stendahl, New York 1957, pp. 94—113. Cf. p. 104. This article originally appeared in ZThK 49 (1952), pp. 200—222.
[22] Cf. Reuben 4 11; Issachar 7 7; Dan 4 7; Asher 1 3-8, 6 5; Benjamin 3 3; Judah 20 1-2; and EGON BRANDENBURGER, Adam und Christus, Neukirchen 1962, pp. 23—25.

as we see in Gal. 4 3-9. In such thought the "elements of the world" take on a demonic aspect and hold men in slavery[23].

In Rom. 6 6ff. Paul connects the motif of dying and rising with Christ to the idea of the two dominions. In fact, he does so even before vs. 6. It is important to recognize that the basic idea of the two dominions, which is developed in vss. 6ff. in connection with the idea of domination by a lord, is expressed by other patterns of thought as well. We must now consider these patterns of thought.

In vs. 2 we find the construction ἀπεθάνομεν τῇ ἁμαρτίᾳ, which reoccurs in vss. 10 and 11 and is contrasted with ζῇ τῷ θεῷ. These datives are usually interpreted as datives of advantage and disadvantage[24]. This is correct as far as it goes, but BLASS-DEBRUNNER, who also treat these constructions under the heading of "Dat. commodi et incommodi," add a remark which is important. After noting that some of Paul's constructions with this dative are very free, they remark with respect to a number of verses, including Rom. 6 10-11, that the dative expresses "mehr den Besitzer."[25] That such an implication is present is clear from the context in Rom. 6, where sin and God, to whose advantage or disadvantage one dies or lives, are not beings of the same level as the one who dies or lives, but are slave masters who rule over men. The connection of this construction with the idea of lordship or ownership is not a peculiarity of this chapter. We also find it in Rom. 14 7-9, where it is explained that we live or die "to the Lord," and this is connected with the fact that "we are the Lord's" and that Christ "exercises lordship over both dead and living."[26] We will note in the course of Part I that this construction occurs in all of the passages in the Pauline homologoumena which refer to dying with Christ as a decisive past event[27], and that this dying is a dying to sin, law, and flesh, the masters which rule over the old world. This use of the dative is the most striking formal consistency of these passages. It makes clear that for Paul dying with Christ means a change of lordship. It means dying to an old master and living to a new one.

In vs. 2 we have another important construction. In the second half of the verse, where we might have expected another simple dative to follow ζήσομεν, we find instead ἐν αὐτῇ. This is another

---

[23] Cf. ALBRECHT OEPKE, Der Brief des Paulus an die Galater, 2. Aufl. Berlin 1957, pp. 93—96, and A. LUMPE, "Elementum," Reallexikon für Antike und Christentum, ed. Theodor Klauser, Stuttgart 1950ff., vol. 4, 1959, col. 1073—1100.

[24] Cf., e. g., SCHNACKENBURG, Heilsgeschehen, p. 28.   [25] Section 188.

[26] Dying "to the Lord" in Rom. 14 8 does not mean the same thing as dying "to sin" in 6 2, for in the latter case this dying means release from subjection. Nevertheless, the dative refers to a master in both cases.

[27] In Gal. 5 25, however, the dative may have more of an instrumental sense.

way in which Paul refers to the dominion of sin, and so has a place within the idea of the two dominions which we are investigating. The importance of this phrase becomes clear when we see that the idea of living "in" sin is part of a broader Pauline pattern of expression. We find similar phrases elsewhere in connection with the contrast between the two dominions. Often it is one of the powers which rules over these dominions which is the object of the preposition. In Gal. 2 17 Paul speaks of being justified "in Christ." This stands in contrast to being justified "in law" (Gal. 3 11, 5 4; Phil. 3 6). This phrase might simply have an instrumental sense. However, Rom. 3 19 shows that it can mean something more than that[28]. There certain people are described simply as "those in the law." This is what characterizes them. This is what determines their existence. The law is related to sin as one of the powers which holds men in bondage in the old aeon (Gal. 3 22—4 7). "Flesh" is another of these powers, and we find the phrase "in flesh" used in a similar way, especially when it is contrasted to existence "in Spirit" (Rom. 8 9, 7 5-6, cf. 2 28-29). The connection of this form of expression to Paul's idea of the two dominions is clear. The two dominions are different because they are ruled by different powers. It is the powers operative in the dominion which determine its nature, which mark it off from another dominion where other powers are operative. Such a dominion is a power field. It is the sphere in which a power is at work. Since Paul sees human existence as being determined by such powers, this existence can be characterized by speaking of it as "in sin," "in law," "in flesh," or "in Spirit."

Paul's use of the phrase "in Christ" is extensive and complex. It is clear, however, that any interpretation of this phrase must give serious attention to its close relation with the phrases discussed in the preceding paragraph, for "in Christ" also refers to action or existence as it is characterized by a particular power, the power of Christ and his saving acts[29]. Thus, it can be used to refer to the new existence of the Christian in contrast to his previous existence in the old dominion (Rom. 8 1-2, II Cor. 5 17, cf. I Cor. 1 30). It is used in this way in Rom. 6 11 and 23, where it is attached to the second member of the contrast between the two dominions, their masters, and their rewards, and indicates that the new life is a reality in the dominion

---

[28] Cf. also Rom. 2 12.
[29] Cf. FRITZ NEUGEBAUER, In Christus, EN ΧΡΙΣΤΩΙ, Göttingen 1961, who emphasizes that "in Christ" means "determined by Christ and his saving acts." NEUGEBAUER interprets the phrase in the light of certain other formulations with ἐν which express an adverbial modification. However, I am not convinced that a local sense can be completely excluded, for Paul seems to connect the idea of determination by a power to the idea of existence within a power sphere.

determined by Christ and his saving acts. In a few passages a further nuance seems to be present. As we will see in the course of this study, Paul can express the fact that existence in the new dominion is determined by Christ and his saving acts by speaking of Christ as a corporate or inclusive person. Those in the new dominion are determined by Christ, for Christ is the new dominion. The phrase "in Christ" is open to this additional sense. Thus in Gal. 3 Paul argues that the believers are "seed of Abraham" because they are included in Christ, the one seed (3 16, 26-29). Those baptized have "put on Christ" (vs. 27). This means that the differences which divided people in the old world have been overcome, for they now form one person. "You are all one (man)[30] in Christ Jesus" (vs. 28). Vs. 27 makes clear that the inclusive unity which the Christians enter is Christ himself, and this is what vs. 28b also wishes to say. They form one person because they are included in Christ, and the phrase "in Christ Jesus" is added just to make this fact clear. The same phrase has the same function in vs. 26. In this sentence it is not the complement of πίστεως[31], for Paul does not use the preposition ἐν to indicate the object of faith[32]. Furthermore, the phrase "in Christ Jesus" is picked up again in vs. 28 in another sense, as we have seen. "In Christ Jesus" is added in vs. 26 to make clear that the status of Christians as sons of God is a derivative one, based on their inclusion in Christ. This is the basic thought in this passage, and in both vss. 26 and 28 the phrase "in Christ Jesus" serves to emphasize this point. We see, then, that this phrase can, on occasion, carry the idea of participation in Christ as inclusive person[33]. In the course of Part I it will be shown that the motif of dying and rising with Christ is also connected with this idea.

In contrast to living in sin (Rom. 6 2), the believers "walk in newness, which consists in life"[34] (vs. 4). Here the eschatological background of the contrast between the two dominions comes out. The sphere in which the believers walk is described as "newness" in contrast to the preceding oldness, i. e., the old aeon. In Rom. 7 6 the two dominions are again referred to in terms of "oldness" and "newness," and we will see that the phrase "our old man" in 6 6 is also involved in this contrast of the two dominions[35].

---

[30] Note the masculine εἷς. Something more than the simple idea of unity is expressed here. Cp. I Cor. 3 8 (neuter).
[31] This connection is rejected in the commentaries by PIERRE BONNARD, ERNEST DEWITT BURTON, ALBRECHT OEPKE, and HEINRICH SCHLIER, *ad loc.*
[32] In Rom. 3 25 ἐν τῷ αὐτοῦ αἵματι modifies ἱλαστήριον. Eph. 1 13, 15 and Col. 1 4 are possible instances, but cf. SCHLIER, *ibid.*   [33] Cf. also I Cor. 15 22, Rom. 12 5.
[34] Epexegetical genitive. So also BORNKAMM, Ende des Gesetzes, p. 38, n. 9.
[35] Cf. pp. 24—30.

c. Romans 6 3-6

The preceding section brought out the importance of the idea of the two dominions in Rom. 6 and investigated some of the patterns of thought by which Paul expresses that idea. The investigation of Paul's use of dying and rising with Christ in Rom. 6 will carry us further into Paul's thought on this point, for Paul connects this motif with the idea of the two dominions. In Rom. 6 Paul is not simply concerned with the two dominions, but with the decisive transfer of the believers from the one dominion to the other. The believers were enslaved to sin, but now they stand under a new master. This change has taken place through dying with Christ. The motif of dying and rising with Christ is important to Paul because it brings out this decisive transfer and connects it to the death and resurrection of Christ. Dying with Christ means dying to the powers of the old aeon and entry into a new life under a new power, as the explanatory comments added in vss. 6-7 and 9-10 to the assertions of vss. 5 and 8 make clear. And this change of lordship is bound up with the death and resurrection of Christ.

But how are we to understand this assertion that the believers have died *with Christ*? This direct connection between the death of Christ and a death on the part of the believers has greatly bothered the interpreters, who have attempted to understand it in various ways. Some point to a relation with the pagan mysteries[36]. Some Roman Catholic scholars develop this relation in a positive manner and speak of the sacramental "presence" of the death and resurrection of Christ in the "cult mystery."[37] Other scholars speak of "passion mysticism."[38] Another refers to a unique possibility of "contemporaneity" with the salvation events by means of the removal of the barriers of time and space[39]. Another emphasizes the present, pneumatic communion of the believer with Christ in a present "salvation event."[40] Others interpret Rom. 6 as a continuation of the

---

[36] Cf., e. g., HANS LIETZMANN, An die Römer, pp. 67—68.
[37] Cf. VIKTOR WARNACH, "Taufe und Christusgeschehen nach Römer 6," Archiv für Liturgiewissenschaft III, 2 (1954), pp. 284—366. WARNACH is following O. CASEL. However, he modifies and limits the idea of derivation from the mysteries considerably. Cf. pp. 327ff. and 339—340, n. 166.
[38] ADOLF DEISSMANN, Paul, pp. 181—83; JOHANNES SCHNEIDER, Die Passionsmystik des Paulus.
[39] WILHELM TRAUGOTT HAHN, Das Mitsterben und Mitauferstehen mit Christus bei Paulus.
[40] RUDOLF SCHNACKENBURG, Das Heilsgeschehen bei der Taufe. Cf. p. 206. In the revised edition of his work, SCHNACKENBURG appeals to the comparison between Adam and Christ and speaks of "corporate personality." Cf. Baptism, pp. 154 ff.

parallel between Adam and Christ in Rom. 5 12-21, understood in terms of "corporate personality."[41] If we are to determine how Paul himself understood this connection between the death of Christ and a death of the believers, we must be careful to be guided by the text. In Rom. 6 3-6 Paul does not speak simply of dying "with Christ," as in vs. 8. He varies his formulations in order to bring out the full scope of the idea with which he is working. These changing but interrelated patterns of thought are our best clue to Paul's understanding of dying with Christ.

We will begin with the idea of baptism εἰς Χριστόν. The interpretation of this phrase has been the subject of considerable controversy. Some interpreters feel that it is necessary to give the εἰς a local sense[42], while others see it as an abbreviated form of εἰς τὸ ὄνομα, and so as a formula for transfer of ownership, or as an indication of the constitutive factor for the nature of the baptismal act or an indication of the goal of this act[43]. The latter kind of interpretation is insufficient. Any interpretation of baptism εἰς Χριστόν must be able to explain how Paul can move from this idea to the related idea of baptism εἰς τὸν θάνατον αὐτοῦ, and then interpret this as participation in Christ's death, as he does in Rom. 6 3ff. Baptism εἰς τὸν θάνατον αὐτοῦ does not simply mean that one is baptized "in the name of his death" or "for his death" or "with reference to his death." Paul explains in vs. 4 that it means that "we were buried with" Christ and in vs. 5 that "we were united with the form of his death." This clearly means that the believer shares in this death, is included in this death. Baptism εἰς Χριστόν must be understood in the same way. It means that through baptism the believer has come to share in Christ. Through baptism he has been included in Christ. He has entered Christ as the corporate person of the new aeon. Thus we should translate: "We were baptized *into* Christ Jesus."

This interpretation will be strengthened when it is shown that this idea of a corporate or inclusive person is present in vs. 6[44]. It can also be supported by a consideration of the other passages in which the phrase βαπτίζω εἰς is used. Paul never refers to baptism "into the name of Christ," though I Cor. 1 13 probably shows that he was acquainted with this formula. He passes over any reference to the "name" of Christ, for he has a different relation in mind. This

---

[41] Cf., e. g., C. H. DODD, The Epistle of Paul to the Romans, London 1932, p. 86.
[42] This goes back at least to W. HEITMÜLLER, Taufe und Abendmahl bei Paulus, Göttingen 1903, p. 9.
[43] Cf., e. g., ALBRECHT OEPKE, TWNT, vol. 1, p. 537 and vol. 2, pp. 430—31; and SCHNACKENBURG, Heilsgeschehen, pp. 19—24.
[44] Cf. pp. 24—25.

is shown by the connection in Gal. 3 27 and I Cor. 12 13 of βαπτίζω εἰς with corporate patterns of thought. In Gal. 3 27ff. baptism into Christ is associated with "putting on Christ" and so being "one in Christ Jesus." This is asserted to show that the believers are "seed of Abraham" because they are included in Christ, the one "seed" (Gal. 3 16, 29). In I Cor. 12 13 we find similar ideas. Here, instead of speaking of baptism into Christ, Paul speaks of baptism "into one body." This body is a unity in which the many individual believers share as members (vs. 12), and so baptism into the one body means that the divisions of the old world have been overcome (vs. 13)[45]. The fact that Paul, in speaking of the body, is speaking of Christ (vs. 12) shows the connection of this passage with Gal. 3 26ff., for baptism into one body also means entry into the inclusive Christ. The fact that baptism into Christ is connected with these ideas of Christ as an inclusive person in Gal. 3 27 and I Cor. 12 13, as well as in Rom. 6 3, gives a good basis for the interpretation of this phrase.

To say that baptism into Christ means entry through baptism into Christ as an inclusive figure is something quite different from saying that Christ as πνεῦμα is equated with the water into which one is plunged in the baptismal rite. I Cor. 10 2 can be used to refute the latter idea[46]. There we have the unusual idea of baptism "into Moses." The idea of a πνεῦμα-Moses would be a strange one. Furthermore, the baptismal medium is given by the added phrase "in the cloud and in the sea," indicating that "into Moses" expresses something else. This formulation corresponds with New Testament usage elsewhere, for the baptismal medium is only once indicated with εἰς (Mark 1 9), but frequently with ἐν. This would indicate that baptism "into Christ" does not presuppose a connection between Christ and the water used in baptism, and has nothing directly to do with the fact that in the rite one enters into the water[47]. While we cannot equate Moses and the baptismal medium in I Cor. 10 2, the interpretation advanced above for baptism "into Christ" provides a suitable explanation of this verse. The idea of baptism "into Moses" is formulated by analogy to baptism "into Christ." Paul is interpreting the old covenant in terms of the new and its sacraments. The fact that the Israelites underwent a baptism and partook of sacramental food which were comparable to the Christian sacraments is important to Paul's argument that the Christian is not guaranteed salvation by these sacraments any more than the Israelites were. In Rom. 5 12-21 Paul contrasts Adam and Christ as the founding figures of the two

---

[45] The same motif occurred at Gal. 3 28.
[46] So SCHNACKENBURG, Heilsgeschehen, pp. 19—20.
[47] Cf. pp. 34—35.

dominions. Each represents in his own person the dominion which he founds. It is possible for Moses, as the founding figure of the old covenant, to take on this same significance. Moses is not merely an individual figure here but represents the whole *Heilsordnung* of the law[48], and to be baptized into him is to enter this sphere of existence.

This survey of all the passages in which Paul uses the construction βαπτίζω εἰς shows a clear connection of this phrase with ideas of an inclusive figure. Therefore, it refers to baptism as entry into Christ, who is an inclusive or corporate person. It is clear in Rom. 6 that this also means entry into the new dominion. We will see below that the idea of Christ as inclusive person is closely related to that of the new dominion in Paul's thought. Christ, as inclusive person, represents and embodies the new dominion in himself. The results of this investigation of baptism "into Christ" are important for understanding what Paul means by dying with Christ. Paul explains that baptism into Christ means baptism into his death. We have found that this is related to ideas of Christ as an inclusive person. The believer participates in Christ's death because he is included in Christ. It is through this connection with inclusive patterns of thought that we must understand dying and rising with Christ.

This is supported by Rom. 6 6. Vs. 6 is not an independent sentence, but is attached to vs. 5 by a participle, and is meant to explain further the significance of the union "with the form of his death" referred to there. In vs. 6 Paul wishes to make clear that this death has freed the believers from slavery to sin, but in explaining this he uses two short clauses which help us to understand how he conceived the death of the believer with Christ. In the one Paul speaks of the crucifixion of "our old man" with Christ; in the other of the destruction of the "body of sin." These phrases do not refer to the "old man" and "body" of each individual, but to a collective entity which is destroyed in the death of Christ. This is made clear, first, by Rom. 7 4 and Col. 2 11. These two verses are closely related to Rom. 6 6, for both make use of the motif of dying and rising with Christ and both connect it with the term σῶμα. It will be demonstrated below that in both these verses this body is at the same time the body which died on the cross and a corporate body in which the believers were included[49]. This body has a negative quality, for redemption takes place through its destruction. It is put to death in Christ's death, and the believers are put to death by means of the death of this body, and so it is understood as a corporate entity. Since we also find reference to the destruction of a body of negative

---

[48] Similarly WARNACH, Archiv für Liturgiewissenschaft III, 2 (1954), p. 328.
[49] Cf. pp. 45—47, 48—50.

quality in connection with dying with Christ in Rom. 6 6, it must be interpreted in the same way. Second, the collective sense of the concepts in Rom. 6 6 is shown by the use of ὁ παλαιὸς ἄνθρωπος elsewhere. This phrase does not occur in the Pauline homologoumena outside of Rom. 6 6, but it does occur in Ephesians and Colossians[50]. Col. 3 9-10 makes clear that the "old man" and his counterpart, the "new man," are corporate concepts. They are realities which the many individuals "strip off" and "put on," just as they "put on" Christ (Gal. 3 27, Rom. 13 14). As there is only one Christ, not a Christ for each individual, so there is only one old man and one new man. Thus putting on the new man binds the many believers into a unity which overcomes the divisions of the world (Col. 3 10-11). Gal. 3 28 associates this same motif with putting on Christ, who is understood as a corporate person[51]. Thus this old man and new man are corporate figures, related to the idea of Christ as a corporate person, and the phrase "our old man" in Rom. 6 6 must be interpreted accordingly. Third, this interpretation is supported by the preceding section of the letter to the Romans. In 5 12-21 Paul compares and contrasts Adam and Christ. These two are not simply men among other men. In each case the act of the one determines the existence of the many. It is this relation between the one and the many which makes this pattern of thought useful to Paul (Cf. 5 18-19). In this section the word ἄνθρωπος has a special significance. The phrase "the one man" is repeated (vss. 12, 19), slipping in even where the proper name is also used (vs. 15). The connection of the term ἄνθρωπος with the ideas being used here is clearer in I Cor. 15. In vss. 45-49 Paul begins from a passage of scripture which uses the term, and then describes Adam and Christ as the first and the second ἄνθρωπος. This ignores all the men that came between them. Evidently Adam and Christ are ἄνθρωποι in a sense that other men are not. This is connected to the fact that these two are determinative for the many. The many "wear" the "image" of the one or the other (vs. 49), and share in their nature, whether earthly or heavenly (vs. 48). This makes clear the connection of the term ἄνθρωπος with the idea of a figure who determines the existence of the many because they share in his nature, so that what is true of the one is true of the many. Thus this "man" sums up the existence of the many. In Rom. 6 6 it is not clear that "our old man" is specifically identified with Adam. However, it is clear that this phrase is connected with the idea of a man who sums up the existence of the many, as do Adam and Christ.

---

[50] On the significance of Eph. and Col. for this study see pp. 47—48.
[51] On Gal. 3 26-29, see p. 20.

Clarification of the relation of Rom. 5 12-21 and Rom. 6 will help us to understand the significance of what we have found. In many respects the contrast between the language and thought-patterns of these two sections of Romans is striking. The idea of dying and rising with Christ, so important in chapter 6, is introduced suddenly, with no preparation in chapter 5. The language of "justification" and "faith," which is so important in Romans up through chapter 5, suddenly becomes less important in chapter 6[52]. However, the connection between the two sections becomes clear if we note the importance of the contrast between the two dominions in both. We have already seen the importance of this contrast in Rom. 6. The same contrast is already developed in Rom. 5 12-21. On the one hand, death and sin "reign" (βασιλεύω: 5 14, 17, 21), and this is contrasted with the reign of grace (vs. 21). The same language is applied to sin in 6 12. Furthermore, these two dominions are connected with Adam and Christ. It is through Adam that sin entered the world and reigns (vss. 12, 21), and it is through Jesus Christ that grace reigns (vs. 21). This is simply an aspect of the fact that the acts of Adam and Christ determine the existence of the many, and so the comparison between the effect of the one act and the effect of the other in vss. 18-19 becomes in vs. 21 a comparison of the reign of sin and the reign of grace. Thus vs. 21 concludes and summarizes the thought of 5 12-21. At the same time it prepares the way for what follows, for this contrast of two reigns is basic to Rom. 6. Thus 5 12-21 provides an introduction for chapter 6, indeed, it lays the foundation for the discussion of sin, law, and death which follows in Rom. 6—8[53].

The connection developed in Rom. 5 12-21 between the two dominions and the two "men," Adam and Christ, enables Paul to bring out clearly the Christological and soteriological foundation of the new dominion. Christ is the founding figure of the new dominion, just as Adam was of the old. More specifically, Christ's *act* is the foundation of the new dominion, just as Adam's act was the foundation of the old. This is made clear in Rom. 5 18-19. In these verses the parallel between Adam and Christ is developed by comparing, on the one hand, the effect of Adam's "transgression" and "disobedience," and, on the other hand, the effect of Christ's "righteous act" and "obedience." This "righteous act" and "obedience" refer primarily to Jesus' death. Paul seldom concerns himself with the ethical quality of Jesus' life. Instead, he focuses his attention on the

---

[52] It is not completely absent. Δικαιόω and πιστεύω occur in vss. 7 and 8, but not in the full senses which Paul gives them elsewhere. Δικαιοσύνη becomes an important term from vs. 13 on.

[53] Cf. EGON BRANDENBURGER Adam und Christus, pp. 255ff.

saving events of the cross and resurrection[54]. This is the case here also, as is shown by the parallel with Adam, for Adam's disobedience was not a matter of the quality of his life as a whole, but of one crucial act, his transgression of a particular command. Through Adam's transgression the reign of death was established (vs. 17). Christ's "righteous act" has a similar significance (cf. vss. 18-19, 21). These two acts are the founding acts of the two dominions. Since Christ's "righteous act" brings to an end the reign of sin and death and establishes the new dominion, it is closely connected to the idea of dying with Christ in Rom. 6, which also refers to release from the old dominion and transfer to the new. Furthermore, Paul develops his thought in 5 12-21 by speaking of two corporate "men." Of each of these two men it may be said: as the one, so the many (cf. I Cor. 15 48). Each determines the existence of the many, so that the fate of these many is tied up with his own fate. To go on to say that the determinative acts of the two corporate men are themselves corporate or inclusive acts is only a small step from this. But Paul could not easily take this step within the confines of the parallel between Adam and Christ. To develop his thought further he needed to be able to refer explicitly to the death and resurrection of Christ, not simply to his "righteous act," and to make clear that these events are inclusive events through which the believer himself dies to the old dominion and lives under a new master. For this purpose Paul takes up the motif of dying and rising with Christ. Thus this motif serves to develop further the thought of Rom. 5 12-21, and applies it to the important question of the Christian's relation to sin. Paul understands the basic patterns of thought of these two sections of Romans as aspects of one train of thought. Rom. 6 6 is of special importance because it makes this relation clear, giving us an important clue as to how Paul understood dying with Christ and how it is to be related to the rest of his thought.

Although Rom. 6 6 is related to 5 12-21 through reference to an inclusive *anthropos*, this verse implies something more than what we find in that passage. In 5 12-21 Adam and Christ are contrasted. In 6 6 the "old man" is crucified with Christ, which implies that Christ is related to this "old man." Indeed, the fact that the "old man" and the "body of sin" are destroyed in Christ's crucifixion seems to imply that Christ is the bearer of this inclusive reality of the old aeon. This may seem surprising, but it is not an isolated idea in

---

[54] The reference to the fact that Christ did not "know sin" in II Cor. 5 21 may be occasioned by the requirement for a sacrifice without blemish (cf. Hebr. 9 14, I Peter 1 19), for it is only the presupposition for the fact that God "made" him "sin." Phil. 2 8 refers to Christ's obedience, but this culminates in his death on the cross.

Paul's writings. It is made clear elsewhere that Christ in his earthly life stands under the powers of the old aeon. He is subject to death (Rom. 6 9), to sin (Rom. 6 10), to the archons (I Cor. 2 8), and to the law, which at the same time means being under the "elemental powers of the world" (Gal. 4 3-5). Thus Christ shares fully in the existence of the old aeon. Furthermore, we will see that the idea of Christ on the cross bearing the inclusive reality of the old aeon, which is thereby destroyed, comes out in two other passages which refer to dying and rising with Christ, Rom. 7 4 and Col. 2 11, both in connection with the term σῶμα. Since this body has a negative quality in Rom. 6 6 and Col. 2 11, this implies a sharply negative view of the human existence in the old aeon in which Christ shares.

Other interpreters have asserted that there is a connection between dying and rising with Christ in Rom. 6 and the interpretation of Adam and Christ in Rom. 5 12-21[55]. However, this has not been supported through a careful consideration of Paul's use of dying and rising with Christ. Furthermore, the connection between these ideas does not mean that we can simply interpret Paul's thought from the Old Testament patterns of thought which have been given the title "corporate personality."[56] It has become common for interpreters to apply this term to aspects of Paul's thought, such as the comparison of Adam and Christ, and some have even pointed to a relation with the motif of dying and rising with Christ[57]. However, the term "corporate personality," when applied to Paul, covers up a lot of problems. If it is understood to refer to Old Testament conceptions of the solidarity of the tribe or nation, a solidarity which could be manifested through one person who is representative of the whole, then this has something to contribute to our understanding of Paul but is not a sufficient explanation of Paul's corporate or inclusive

---

[55] C. H. DODD, Romans, p. 86; ANDERS NYGREN, Commentary on Romans, Philadelphia 1949, pp. 232—33, 237—38.

[56] For the meaning of this phrase see H. WHEELER ROBINSON, "The Hebrew Conception of Corporate Personality," Werden und Wesen des Alten Testaments, ed. Johannes Hempel, Berlin 1936, pp. 49—62.

[57] ERNEST BEST, One Body in Christ, London 1955, attempts to show the unity of Paul's inclusive terminology by tracing it all back to this idea of corporate personality. RUDOLF SCHNACKENBURG, "Todes- und Lebensgemeinschaft mit Christus: Neue Studien zu Röm. 6 1-11," Münchener Theologische Zeitschrift 6 (1955), pp. 32—53, applies this idea to Rom. 6. See also Baptism, pp. 154 ff. Others who use this idea to interpret Paul include: TRAUGOTT SCHMIDT, Der Leib Christi, Leipzig 1919, pp. 223—236; C. H. DODD, Romans, pp. 79 ff., 86; ERNST PERCY, Der Leib Christi in den paulinischen Homologumena und Antilegomena, Lund 1942, pp. 38 bis 43, and Die Probleme der Kolosser- und Epheserbriefe, Lund 1946, pp. 108 bis 109; J. DE FRAINE, Adam et son Lignage, Bruges 1959, pp. 193—225; RUSSELL PHILIP SHEDD, Man in Community, London 1958, pp. 93 ff.

patterns of thought. Jewish thought about Adam is not a simple continuation of Old Testament ideas of corporate personality, but shows definite speculative aspects which reveal other forces at work[58]. Furthermore, Paul's interpretation of Adam and Christ has important aspects which are not derived from Old Testament thought[59]. In I Cor. 15 45-49 Adam and Christ are associated with a sharp dualism of earthly and heavenly, ψυχικός and πνευματικός. This dualism cannot be explained by referring to corporate personality. The ideas in these verses did not originate in Paul's mind, for he is dependent on a tradition. This is made clear by vs. 45, which quotes Gen. 2 7 as if it referred to two Adams. This quotation, and the argument based upon it, would only be acceptable to those who already accepted this particular interpretation of Gen. 2 7. Furthermore, the correction which Paul makes in vs. 46 only makes sense if it is directed against someone who has employed the same terms, but in the reverse order. Finally, there are a number of words in these verses which are not part of Paul's usual vocabulary[60]. Evidently they are part of the tradition which he is using. The fact that Paul is influenced by such a dualistic tradition makes clear that the historical background of Paul's thought is more complicated than is assumed when it is understood in terms of Old Testament corporate personality. We can find ideas related to the tradition which Paul uses in I Cor. 15 45-49. We find them not in the Old Testament or in aspects of Jewish thought which remain close to the Old Testament, but in gnostic texts[61] and in Philo[62].

What we have discovered so far gives us some insight into what Paul means when he says that the believer has died with Christ. The believers died with Christ because Christ's crucifixion meant the crucifixion of "our old man" and the "body of sin." These are corporate entities. They are associated with slavery to sin, as Rom. 6 6

---

[58] Cf. WILLI STAERK, Die Erlösererwartung in den östlichen Religionen (Soter II), Stuttgart 1938, pp. 7—21, and EGON BRANDENBURGER, Adam und Christus, p. 138.
[59] This is brought out well by BRANDENBURGER.
[60] Cf. BRANDENBURGER, p. 76, n. 1.
[61] Cf. the tradition which is found in varying forms in Irenaeus, Adversus haereses I, 24, 1 and I, 30, 6; Hippolytus, Refutatio omnium haeresium V, 7, 6—8; "Das Wesen der Archonten" 135, 12—136, 18, translated by HANS-MARTIN SCHENKE, ThLZ 83 (1958), col. 661—670; and the "Apocryphon of John" 47, 14ff., translated in R. M. GRANT, Gnosticism, New York 1961, pp. 77ff. This tradition speaks of the formation of an earthly man in the "image" of the "Power above," who can also be called "Man." It is connected with a particular interpretation of Gen. 1 26 and 2 7.
[62] Cf. Legum Allegoria I, 31. Such *anthropos*-speculation is found in many passages in Philo. Again, it is especially connected with the interpretation of Gen. 1 26 and 2 7.

shows, and so we may say that they refer to the old dominion as a corporate entity. When the believers were in slavery to sin, they were part of this inclusive "old man;" their existence was bound up with his. Therefore, the destruction of the "old man" in the cross of Christ meant the death of the believers as men of the old aeon. Paul is not speaking of the death of individual believers one by one. He is speaking of the destruction of the dominion of sin, of which all believers were a part. Baptism has an important place in Paul's thought in Rom. 6, but what takes place in baptism is founded upon what has taken place in Christ's death[63]. This foundation is brought out in vs. 6. There Paul is not referring to the variety of times when the believers were baptized. He is referring to the one time of Christ's death on the cross. Christ's cross puts an end to the dominion of sin, and so to the "old man." It is an inclusive event, for the existence of men was bound up with this old aeon, and what puts an end to it also puts an end to them as men of the old aeon. When Paul speaks of dying and rising with Christ, and associates it, as he does here, with the end of the old dominion and the foundation of the new, it is clear that he is thinking of the death and resurrection of Christ as eschatological events. And because they are eschatological events, affecting the old dominion as a whole, they are also inclusive events.

The importance of these observations can be briefly indicated here[64]. If this interpretation is correct, dying and rising with Christ cannot be understood as a repetition of Christ's death and resurrection, or as the result of some subjective or sacramental process by which Christ's death and resurrection are made present, or in any other way which seeks to supplement the death and resurrection of Christ as particular events in the past and thereby make up their deficiencies. Provided that dying and rising with Christ is understood in the context of Paul's eschatology, it is clear both that the death and resurrection of Christ are particular, past events and that the believers participate in them, for these events involve the old and new dominions as wholes, and so also those who are included in these dominions.

Some interpreters find indication of a different interpretation in Rom. 6 5. We must now turn to this difficult and much-discussed verse. According to one interpretation, it is necessary to supply αὐτῷ after σύμφυτοι γεγόναμεν and to take τῷ ὁμοιώματι as instrumental dative or dative of reference. To supply another dative when there is already a dative present which could complete the construction is

---

[63] Cf. pp. 41—43.
[64] Cf. further pp. 39—43, 70—74.

not an easy interpretation to support, especially when the word to be supplied is only found some distance away, at the beginning of vs. 4. Furthermore, Paul is not concerned in this chapter with communion with Christ in general (as would be the case if we supply αὐτῷ), but with participation in his death and resurrection, through which the believer is released from the dominion of sin. The strongest argument for supplying αὐτῷ seems to be that advanced by SCHNAKKENBURG in his first treatment of this problem. He asserts, "Entscheidend aber ist, daß die Vokabel σύμφυτοι eine organische Verbindung verlangt, hier also mit einer Person."[65] Later he adds, "Auch auf den anorganischen Bereich erstreckt sich die Anwendungsmöglichkeit der Vokabel; aber nur *Gleichartiges* kann durch συμφύειν verbunden werden."[66] However, OTTO KUSS has shown that this assertion cannot be supported by the actual usage of σύμφυτος[67], and SCHNACKENBURG himself has given up this interpretation[68].

HEINRICH SCHWARZMANN denies that τῷ ὁμοιώματι is the complement of σύμφυτοι without supplying an αὐτῷ[69]. He takes the genitive τοῦ θανάτου αὐτοῦ as the complement of σύμφυτοι and interprets τῷ ὁμοιώματι as an instrumental dative. The "likeness" is, then, the baptismal rite, by means of which the believer dies with Christ. BLASS-DEBRUNNER mention this as a possibility, but they also give the decisive argument against it: "Doch ist die Verbindung des Gen. mit dem vorangehenden Wort natürlicher, und ὁμοίωμα hat sonst bei Paul. immer einen Gen."[70] SCHWARZMANN tries to accommodate his argument to this fact by asserting that τοῦ θανάτου αὐτοῦ is also to be supplied after ὁμοίωμα, but was omitted to avoid repeating the phrase twice in a row[71]. Such confusion is avoided by abandoning SCHWARZMANN's interpretation. Furthermore, the word order speaks decisively against this view. If Paul wished to say what SCHWARZMANN thinks he wished to say, he would have had to make clear through the word order that τοῦ θανάτου αὐτοῦ and not τῷ ὁμοιώματι was the complement of σύμφυτοι, for otherwise the reader would naturally take the next possible word as such a complement. SCHWARZMANN does not see this because he believes that it is simply impossible to take τῷ ὁμοιώματι as the complement of σύμφυτοι. To support this he uses the argument given by SCHNACKENBURG

---

[65] Heilsgeschehen, p. 41.
[66] *Ibid.*, p. 43. This argument goes back to ERNST KÜHL, Römer, p. 204.
[67] Römerbrief, p. 300.
[68] Cf. Münchener Theologische Zeitschrift 6 (1955), pp. 32—53.
[69] Zur Tauftheologie des hl. Paulus in Röm. 6, Heidelberg 1950.
[70] Section 194, 2.
[71] p. 40.

above[72]. However, we have seen that this argument cannot be accepted.

From the refutation of the two positions above it is clear that we must translate vs. 5a in this way: "If we have become united[73] with τῷ ὁμοιώματι of his death . . ." But what ὁμοίωμα means in this sentence remains a major problem. Some interpreters explain this word as the result of a mixture of more than one idea in vs. 5. In other words, Paul is not expressing himself clearly. KARL MITTRING believes that it is caused by the mixture of dying with Christ with the ὥσπερ-οὕτως pattern of thought of vs. 4b[74]. But Paul is not expressing a different thought in vs. 4b than elsewhere in the chapter. The formulation there is caused by the fact that Paul, in line with his basic concern, does not speak simply of rising with Christ, which can be expressed with a συν- verb, but of walking in newness of life, and yet wishes to bring out the connection between this new life and Christ's resurrection. "*Walking with* Christ in newness of life" would not express what Paul wished to say, and so he changes to a comparison. Though this by itself would be open to the misunderstanding that the believers are only doing something *similar* to what happened to Christ, in this context it is clear that the connection between Christ's resurrection and the believer's newness of life is a deeper one. Therefore, vs. 4b does not express a thought which could be the occasion for the word ὁμοίωμα in vs. 5. Neither in vs. 4b nor, as we shall see, in vs. 5 does Paul weaken the connection between Christ's death and resurrection and the death and resurrection of the believer to only a likeness.

There are other variations on the idea that Paul has not expressed himself clearly. LIETZMANN remarks, "Verkürzte und daher logisch ungenaue Ausdrucksform für 'wenn wir durch die Nachbildung seines Todes mit seinem Tode zusammengewachsen sind.'"[75] This interpretation is the result of seeing that τῷ ὁμοιώματι must be connected directly to σύμφυτοι, and yet refusing to give up the idea that it refers to the baptismal rite and has instrumental sense.

There is another interpretation in which τῷ ὁμοιώματι is seen as referring to the baptismal rite which does not involve asserting that Paul is not really saying what he means. VIKTOR WARNACH argues that ὁμοίωμα, in contrast to ὁμοιότης and ὁμοίωσις, means "Gleichheit im Sinne konkreter Gegenständlichkeit," rather than the

---

[72] SCHWARZMANN, pp. 35—36.

[73] The original sense of this word ("grown together") may no longer be felt. Cf. Kuss, Römerbrief, p. 300, and MYLES M. BOURKE, A Study of the Metaphor of the Olive Tree in Romans XI, Washington, D. C. 1947, pp. 112—124.

[74] Heilswirklichkeit bei Paulus, Gütersloh 1929, p. 48.

[75] Römer, p. 68. Cf. also ERNST PERCY, Der Leib Christi, p. 27.

abstract idea of "likeness." Thus it can stand for "das 'Gleichgemachte' bzw. das 'Abbild.'"[76] Since Paul is speaking in Rom. 6 of the baptismal cult, this concrete "likeness" must refer to the "Kultsymbol."[77] Of course, Paul is asserting that the believer has been united with Christ's death, not with the baptismal rite. But the baptismal "likeness," as a genuine *symbol*, contains the original reality of which it is a symbol, and makes it present. "Somit ist das ὁμοίωμα in der Taufe die kultsymbolische Erscheinung und Gegenwart göttlicher bzw. heilsgeschichtlicher Wirklichkeit, genauerhin, des Christusgeschehens selbst."[78]

There are some important objections to this interpretation of ὁμοίωμα in Rom. 6 5. Ellipsis is common in Paul, and in vs. 5b it is clear that Paul intends the reader to supply the parts of the first clause which have been omitted in the second, among them τῷ ὁμοιώματι. If this is the case, the future verb indicates that the τῷ ὁμοιώματι to be supplied in vs. 5b cannot refer to the presence of the Christ event in the past baptismal rite, and so neither can the parallel use of ὁμοίωμα in the first half of the verse. Even if this were only a logical future, as some believe[79], it is strange that Paul would have to argue for the union of the believer with the ὁμοίωμα of Christ's resurrection if this ὁμοίωμα is directly connected with baptism, for then this union would be attested by the baptismal event itself. WARNACH, seeing this difficulty, denies that anything at all is to be supplied in vs. 5b. He interprets the genitive as a genitive of possession and translates, "So werden wir aber auch der Auferstehung (zugehörig) sein." In supporting this he asserts that for Paul the resurrection is "eine objektive Wirklichkeit oder Macht ..., der man sehr wohl angehören kann."[80] It would not be impossible for Paul to say what WARNACH asserts he is saying — in another context. But it is a strained interpretation of this verse. It requires a sudden wrenching of the pattern of thought, so that in the first half of the verse Paul refers to the ὁμοίωμα of Christ's death as something with which we are united, but in the second half suddenly speaks of the resurrection as something to which we belong. The words which appear in vs. 5b are precisely those which must be changed from the first half of the verse. The elements of the first clause which remain the same in the second are those which are not expressed. It is most natural, then, to interpret vs. 5b as parallel to

---

[76] "Taufe und Christusgeschehen nach Römer 6," Archiv für Liturgiewissenschaft III, 2 (1954), p. 304. Cf. PETER BRUNNER, Aus der Kraft des Werkes Christi, München 1950, pp. 21ff., 68ff.   [77] WARNACH, pp. 306—07.
[78] *Ibid.*, p. 310. Cf. also JOHANNES SCHNEIDER, TWNT, vol. 5, pp. 194—95.
[79] Against this view see pp. 10—12.
[80] p. 313.

5a, and this means that ὁμοίωμα cannot refer to something which is restricted to the past baptismal rite.

The same conclusion is indicated by a consideration of vs. 5a alone. While Paul uses aorist verbs in vss. 3-4, in vs. 5 he changes to a perfect. This perfect takes in the past, punctiliar event to which the aorists referred and asserts the continuing existence of the resultant relationship[81]. Therefore, being united with the ὁμοίωμα of Christ's death is not restricted to the past rite, but is something which is characteristic of the continuing existence of the Christian. It is clear that the ὁμοίωμα of Christ's death with which the Christian has been united is not something which is uniquely connected with the baptismal rite.

The interpretation of τῷ ὁμοιώματι as a reference to the baptismal rite has been furthered by the belief that vss. 3-5, when referring to death, burial, and resurrection, connect these to the separate parts of the rite[82]. However, this is not as certain as many interpreters seem to think. There is no clear analogy between the act of entering the water and Christ's death, for Christ was not drowned. Nor is there a clear analogy between entering the water and burial, for burial at sea is not the normal means of burial. It is likely that Paul speaks of burial with Christ not because the one baptized goes down beneath the water, but in order to emphasize the reality and finality of the believer's death. The reference to burial thus has a function similar to the reference to Christ's burial in the tradition cited in I Cor. 15 3ff., and may have been suggested by the presence of this element in tradition[83]. This interpretation not only fits in well with Paul's argument in this chapter, which depends on the finality of the believer's death to sin, but also is supported by the inferential οὖν which relates vs. 4 to vs. 3. If burial with Christ were something attested by the very form of the baptismal rite, one would expect Paul to use this fact to support his preceding assertion, and instead of οὖν we would have γάρ, an emendation actually attested by the Vulgate, some of the old Latin manuscripts, and Origen. Instead, Paul moves from the assertion that we were baptized into Christ's death to the inference that we were buried with him, i. e., that this was a full and final separation from the old life. Furthermore, the reference to baptism into Christ and his death in vss. 3-4 does not result from reflection on the believer's entry into the water, for we

---

[81] BLASS-DEBRUNNER, sections 318, 4 and 340.
[82] Cf. LIETZMANN, Römer, p. 65; MARTIN DIBELIUS, Botschaft und Geschichte, vol. 2, Tübingen 1956, p. 143.
[83] Cf. EDUARD STOMMEL, "'Begraben mit Christus' (Röm. 6 4) und der Taufritus," Römische Quartalschrift für christliche Altertumskunde und Kirchengeschichte 49 (1954), pp. 1—20; BORNKAMM, Ende des Gesetzes, p. 38.

have already seen that Christ and his death are not equated with the baptismal water by this pattern of thought[84]. The assertion that the details of the baptismal rite determine the development of Paul's thought in vss. 3-5 has little to commend it, therefore, and it is impossible to interpret the ὁμοίωμα of vs. 5 on this basis. We must, then, reject the interpretation of ὁμοίωμα as referring to the baptismal rite in its symbolic significance.

It is now necessary to give an alternative interpretation of ὁμοίωμα in Rom. 6 5. JOHANNES SCHNEIDER points out that there are two basic meanings of ὁμοίωμα in the LXX, copy or image ("Abbild") and form ("Gestalt")[85]. He understands Rom. 6 5 in terms of the former meaning and refers ὁμοίωμα to the baptismal rite in the manner of WARNACH. Since we have found that this interpretation is unacceptable, we must consider the other possible meaning of this word. In this meaning ὁμοίωμα indicates the form of the reality itself in its outward appearance, rather than a second thing which is similar to this reality. This would mean that Rom. 6 5 does not refer to the union of the believers with a "likeness" of Christ's death which is distinct from that death, but rather speaks of a direct union with Christ's death. This interpretation is to be preferred.

If this is so, why does Paul speak of the "form" of Christ's death rather than speaking simply of his death? This is a difficult question, but an answer can at least be suggested. In Phil. 2 7 the word ὁμοίωμα is used to describe the existence of Christ after his self-emptying. He was born ἐν ὁμοιώματι ἀνθρώπων. This phrase must be understood in the light of the parallel statement: μορφὴν δούλου λαβών. This does not mean that Christ merely appeared like a slave. It means a real participation in slave existence. This is shown by the fact that existence in the "form of a slave" stands in contrast to a previous existence "in the form of God." If μορφή indicates that Christ was only a slave in outward appearance, then it must also indicate that he was only divine in outward appearance. But then the statement that "he emptied himself" makes no sense. Since the "form of God" and the "form of a slave" are separated by this self-emptying, the former must refer to a real participation in divine existence and the latter to a real participation in the existence of a slave[86]. The phrase ἐν ὁμοιώματι ἀνθρώπων must be

---

[84] Cf. pp. 22—24.

[85] TWNT, vol. 5, p. 191. For clear examples of the latter meaning see Deut. 4 12, 15; Ezek. 1 16.

[86] Cf. ERNST KÄSEMANN, "Kritische Analyse von Phil. 2 5-11," Exegetische Versuche und Besinnungen, vol. 1, Göttingen 1960, pp. 65ff. He argues that μορφή indicates here "nicht die Eigenart oder Erscheinungsweise oder Haltung, sondern

interpreted in a similar way. The whole hymn is characterized by a pleonastic style. To see a distinction here between μορφή and ὁμοίωμα is to overinterpret the text[87]. The fact that Christ was "born in the form of men" merely makes clearer that "taking the form of a slave" involves entering human existence. The contrast between Christ's divine existence and his human existence as a slave is essential to the main emphasis on his self-emptying and self-humiliation. Vs. 7 does not intend to weaken this by implying that Christ was a man in appearance only. Thus both μορφή and ὁμοίωμα refer here not to an outward likeness but to a particular "form" of existence.

In Rom. 8 3 we find ὁμοίωμα used in a setting similar to that of Phil. 2 7. Here also it is a matter of the sending of the pre-existent Son into the world, and the occurrence of the same term suggests that we are dealing with a pattern of thought which carries with it a set terminology of which ὁμοίωμα is a part. In Rom. 8 3 the Son is sent into the world ἐν ὁμοιώματι σαρκὸς ἁμαρτίας. This "flesh of sin" refers to human existence in the old aeon, where sin is the dominating power. It is related to the "body of sin" (Rom. 6 6) and the "body of the flesh" (Col. 2 11) which Christ bore until it was destroyed in his crucifixion[88]. Texts related to Rom. 8 3 through the motif of the sending of the pre-existent Son make clear that the participation of the Son in the existence of the old aeon serves God's saving purpose. Note the telic constructions in the following passages: the Son was "born under law in order that he might ransom those under law" (Gal. 4 4-5); he "became poor in order that you might become rich by his poverty" (II Cor. 8 9). Similarly, Christ's presence "in the form of the flesh of sin" made possible God's condemnation of "sin in the flesh."[89] The reality of the condemnation of "sin in the flesh" is dependent on the reality of Christ's participation in the "flesh of sin," just as the reality of the ransom of those under law is dependent on the reality of Christ's own existence under law.

There is no reflection in Rom. 8 3 upon whether Christ committed concrete acts of sin. The phrase "flesh of sin" characterizes the world

---

schlechthin das Wesen ..., welches durch das Dasein in einer bestimmten Sphäre charakterisiert wird" (p. 73).

[87] It is also unlikely that σχῆμα means "(only) outward appearance" in vs. 7. Cf. I Cor. 7 31 where σχῆμα indicates simply the "form" of this world. There is no indication that this is merely external and that some deeper reality will remain when "the form of this world passes away."

[88] Cf. pp. 24—25, 27—28, 48—50.

[89] This act of condemnation probably refers to Christ's death. Compare the destruction of the "body of sin" and "body of the flesh" in Christ's death in Rom. 6 6 and Col. 2 11 (cp. Rom. 7 4). Cf. pp. 24—25, 27—28, 48—50.

as a whole in its opposition to the heavenly world from which the Son descended. The sending of the Son "in the form of the flesh of sin" means that he entered this world and shared in its life. Paul was no more afraid to speak of the real existence of Christ within the world determined by the power of sin than of his subjection to the other powers of the old aeon[90]. This is shown by Rom. 6 10, which makes clear that Christ was released by death not only from the dominion of death but also from the dominion of sin. This is not to be refuted by the reference to Christ "not knowing sin" in II Cor. 5 21. This verse can be interpreted in two ways. The fact that Christ was "made sin on our behalf" may refer to Christ's death as a sin offering. Then the reference to his sinlessness can apply to his earthly life. This interest in the sinless quality of Christ's earthly life would be unusual in Paul, and might be occasioned by the requirement of a sacrificial victim "without blemish" (cf. Hebr. 9 14, I Peter 1 19). In that case we are dealing with a pattern of thought which differs from the motif of the sending of the Son into the world and his subjection to the powers, and it would be a mistake to interpret Rom. 8 3 from II Cor. 5 21. On the other hand, it is possible that II Cor. 5 21 does belong to the same circle of ideas as Rom. 8 3. In that case the period of not knowing sin refers to Christ's pre-existence and being made sin for us to the incarnation. Whichever interpretation one prefers (the former is, perhaps, the more likely), the interpretation of Rom. 8 3 above must be allowed to stand. Therefore, ὁμοίωμα here, as in Phil. 2 7, refers to the mode of the Son's existence in the world. This was not merely an outward "likeness" to the flesh of sin, but a real participation in human existence, which is characterized by this flesh of sin.

There is a reason why the words ὁμοίωμα and μορφή appear in Phil. 2 7 and Rom. 8 3. They are part of a theology of metamorphosis, in which two "forms" of existence are contrasted with each other. In the long history in mythology of this idea of the metamorphosis of a divine being[91], it undoubtedly once had the sense of "only in appearance." The human form of the god was only a disguise. But that is no longer the case in these texts. Here the assumption of a different "form" means a self-emptying (Phil. 2 7). It means entering a new sphere of existence, which essentially conditions the mode of

---

[90] For references to Christ's subjection to the powers of the old aeon see pp. 27—28.
[91] MARTIN DIBELIUS remarks with reference to μορφή: "Das Wort hat in Beziehung auf Götter und Gott eine fast selbstverständliche mythische Bedeutung: es bezeichnet die göttliche Gestalt, die der Gott gelegentlich mit einer menschlichen vertauscht." An die Thessalonicher I, II, An die Philipper, 3. Aufl. Tübingen 1937, p. 74.

existence[92]. The terminology of metamorphosis continues, though this transformation has taken on a new meaning.

We have seen above that ὁμοίωμα can be used by Paul as a synonym of μορφή, and that both these terms can be connected with the idea of transformation. Paul also uses compounds of μορφή to speak of transformation. The texts which use the terms σύμμορφος, συμμορφίζομαι, μεταμορφόω and εἰκών refer to a transformation of the believers from earthly to heavenly existence through taking on the same form as the risen Christ[93]. Since this is a transformation of the *believers* which is at the same time a *conformation* to Christ, Paul's thought in these texts is closely related to that in Rom. 6 5. In fact, this conformation to the risen Christ is essentially the same thing as being "united with the form of his resurrection." The relation is made fully clear by Phil. 3 10, where this idea of conformation is joined to that of dying with Christ. There we find: συμμορφιζόμενος τῷ θανάτῳ αὐτοῦ. Except for the significant change in tense (present instead of perfect), this phrase expresses essentially the same thought as Rom. 6 5a. In each case the idea of "form" is connected with a reference to participation in Christ's death.

It is now possible to offer an interpretation of the significance of ὁμοίωμα in Rom. 6 5. In Phil. 2 7 and Rom. 8 3 this term is connected with the two forms or modes of Christ's existence. Paul may use this term in Rom. 6 5 because the death and resurrection are connected with the two "forms" of Christ's existence, the earthly existence of the one who was subject to the powers and the heavenly existence of the exalted Lord. However, the passages which speak of the conformation of the believers to Christ are more closely related to Rom. 6 5. These passages make clear that the believer participates in the "form" of Christ, which means both conformation to the glory of his resurrection (Phil. 3 21) and to his death (Phil. 3 10). The passages which speak of conformation to Christ also make clear that the believers take on Christ's "form" because it is present to them in transforming power[94]. The use of ὁμοίωμα in Rom. 6 5 reflects this idea of conformation to Christ. It adds to the thought of this verse in that it suggests that Christ's death and resurrection are continuing aspects of the "form" of Christ and that the death and

---

[92] KÄSEMANN points to an important change in the meaning of μορφή in Hellenistic times, for in certain Hellenistic religious documents, in contrast to earlier Greek thought, μορφή means "Daseinsweise." Exegetische Versuche, pp. 65ff. Cf. Corpus Hermeticum I, 12.

[93] Rom. 8 29, II Cor. 3 18, Phil. 3 21. Cf. I Cor. 15 49, which should be compared with the two "forms" of existence in Phil. 2 6-7.

[94] This will be shown when these passages are treated in detail on pp. 104—112.

resurrection of Christ are present to the believers in transforming power, so that the believers take on the same "form."

This argument shows that Paul is thinking in Rom. 6 5 of an immediate connection of the believer with the death of Christ. Ὁμοίωμα does not indicate some intervening reality, but is to be taken together with τοῦ θανάτου αὐτοῦ as one phrase, adding to the thought of Christ's death the nuances indicated above. It is clear from the perfect verb that this participation in the death of Christ is a continuing aspect of Christian existence. The "form of his death" is a present reality within the new dominion founded upon Christ's death. The present aspect of participation in Christ's death comes out strongly in the texts which will be treated in Part II under the heading "Dying and Rising with Christ as the Structure of the New Life." It is important for showing the unity of the two parts that this aspect appears also in a passage which primarily speaks of dying with Christ as a past event.

d. Conclusion

A summary of some of our conclusions from the study of Rom. 6 will help us to understand the basis of Paul's assertion that the believer dies with Christ. When Paul speaks of dying and rising with Christ, he is referring to Christ's death and resurrection as eschatological events. As such, they concern the old and new aeons. Through this death and resurrection the believers are freed from the old aeon and the new aeon is founded. Paul thinks of an aeon or dominion as a unified sphere which is ruled by certain powers which determine the character of existence there. The old aeon and the new aeon each form one unit even though they extend over a period of time, for existence in each continues to be determined by the same powers and the same founding events. Because the existence of all within an aeon is based upon and determined by the founding events, the whole of the aeon shares in these events. The inclusive terminology which appears in connection with dying and rising with Christ has a similar sense. This terminology may have its background in non-eschatological myth, but Paul understands it in the context of his eschatology. Christ as inclusive man is the aeon-man of the new aeon, just as Adam was of the old. He is the one who represents and embodies the whole of the new aeon because he determines the nature of existence there. Therefore, the fact of temporal distance creates no major problem for Paul in connection with dying and rising with Christ. He does not isolate individuals from the power sphere in which they exist[95] and he does not think of a series of isolated moments of time, which then must somehow be related. Even major changes in world history would not raise the problem of the believer's isolation from the saving events for Paul, for the new dominion is not an epoch of world history, which could be superseded in the course of historical development, but something which is hidden within history. Within the new dominion past and present form one whole because present existence continues to be determined by the events on which it is founded.

This does not mean that time is of no importance in the new dominion. Time does not separate the believer from Christ's death and resurrection because the new dominion as a whole participates in these events. However, the believer has his particular time and place, and it is the believer in his particular time and place who shares in the cross and resurrection. If this were not so, the cross and resurrection would not determine his concrete life in history, for the believer would be plucked out of history. The passages to be discussed in Part II will make abundantly clear that Paul does not think in this way. Since this is so, we must recognize that the believer's participation in the cross and resurrection may be viewed from two perspectives. When Paul speaks of the foundation of the Christian life in the saving events, differences in time and place are not essential. A particular time and place may become important in the application of Paul's thought, but he can speak first of all concerning the new dominion as a whole. He then emphasizes what has taken place through the past events of Christ's death and resurrection, which are understood as inclusive events in which the whole dominion has participated. But we can also ask: how does this participation in Christ's death and resurrection manifest itself concretely in the individual's life? At this point particular times and places after Christ's resurrection become important. We must speak of the individual's baptism, of faith[96], of particular situations of suffering[97]. In these connections it is proper to speak of the "presence" of the death and resurrection of Christ in the new dominion. This might seem to conflict with the idea that Christ's death and resurrection are inclusive events, which implies that the new dominion was "present" in these past events. However, for Paul these are complimentary aspects of the one motif of dying and rising with Christ. Both make clear that Christian life is determined by participation in Christ's death and resurrection, the one aspect by indicating that the new dominion as a whole participates in these events, the

---

[95] Cf. pp. 71—72.
[96] Cf. pp. 123—26.   [97] Cf. pp. 84 ff.

other by indicating that the life of the individual believer, in its particular time and place, is determined by this participation. Neither of these aspects may be lost if we are to understand what Paul means by dying and rising with Christ[98].

The interpretation of Paul's thought to this point makes clear that dying and rising with Christ cannot be adequately explained by referring to some special quality of the sacrament of baptism. To be sure, this motif was connected with baptism in the tradition of which Paul was a part and this connection continued to be important to Paul. However, for Paul, the death and resurrection of Christ are not present only in baptism. This will be made clear by the passages discussed in Part II, which show that the continuing life of the believer is characterized by participation in Christ's death and resurrection. We have already seen that the union with the form of Christ's death of which Paul speaks in Rom. 6 5 continues after baptism and that this is related to the conformation to Christ's death which takes place in the life of the believer through suffering (Phil. 3 10). Since the death and resurrection of Christ are not present only in baptism, the fact of this presence cannot be attributed to a unique quality of the sacrament of baptism. Indeed, the presence of the death of Christ in baptism is merely one aspect of the presence of the death of Christ in the new dominion as a whole.

However, the participation in Christ's death which takes place in the ongoing life of the believer is based upon a decisive, past death with Christ[99], and it might be argued that baptism is the foundation of the believer's death and resurrection with Christ. At this point clarification is necessary. Baptism, and the decision of faith which accompanies it[100], are decisive events in the life of the individual. The individual is baptized "into Christ" and "into his death," that is, through baptism he enters the new dominion which is determined by Christ and his saving acts[101]. This means that he has been "buried with" Christ, that is, through baptism into Christ's death he has been fully and finally separated from the old life[102]. This entry into Christ and separation from the old life of slavery to

---

[98] The basis of Paul's assertion that the believer dies with Christ is discussed further on pp. 123—27.
[99] Cf. pp. 80—81.
[100] On the relation of faith to dying with Christ see pp. 123—26.
[101] On baptism "into Christ" see pp. 22—24. Entry into Christ as the corporate person of the new aeon is an important aspect of Paul's understanding of baptism, for in the few passages in which Paul both refers explicitly to baptism and gives some explanation of this event this idea predominates. Cf. Rom. 6 3, I Cor. 12 13, Gal. 3 27-28.
[102] Cf. p. 34.

sin is the same transfer from the old dominion to the new dominion which has previously been discussed in connection with the idea of the cross as the eschatological event. Thus in referring to this decisive change Paul can appeal to baptism in Rom. 6. However, this does not mean that we can explain dying with Christ by referring to a special quality of the sacrament of baptism. The believer is baptized into Christ's death and released from the old dominion not because baptism repeats Christ's death or enables it to be present in some unique way, but because in baptism the destruction of the old world and founding of the new which the cross brings about reaches its goal in the life of the individual. Thus baptism does not have an independent significance, supplementing the significance of the cross, for it is the point of fulfillment in the life of the individual of what God is working through the cross. What takes place in baptism is a manifestation of the power of the cross. The individual can enter into Christ and be separated from the old dominion of sin through baptism only because of the eschatological significance of the cross. It is only because it is the effect of Christ's cross to bring the old dominion to an end and establish a new dominion that baptism can mean the realization of this eschatological change in the life of the individual. The motif of dying and rising with Christ, and the corporate patterns of thought associated with it, were connected with baptism in the early church[103]. This connection is important for Paul not because baptism first makes possible such participation in Christ's death, but because the participation in Christ's death which is realized in the life of the individual through baptism is based upon the primal reality of the cross as an eschatological and inclusive event. When Paul speaks of baptism into Christ as baptism into his death in Rom. 6 3, he does not mean that Christ and his death have somehow become lost in the past but are made present through baptism. Rather, this formulation presupposes that, quite apart from the baptism of any particular individual, Christ and his death are continuing realities within the new dominion, so that entry into the new dominion means entry into Christ and his death. One can be baptized into Christ and his death only because the new dominion, which continues to be determined by Christ and his death and to participate in them, has already been established. This has taken place through Christ's cross as an eschatological event, and the fact that what happened there continues to have its effect in the lives of individuals shows the continuing power of this event. Therefore, although baptism has an important place in the concrete realization in the life of the individual believer of death to the old

---

[103] Cf. pp. 7—14, 52—54.

dominion and entry into the new, the possibility of such death with Christ to the old dominion is not based upon baptism itself, and so dying with Christ cannot be explained by referring to a special quality of baptism. Rather, Paul's understanding of the cross is the foundation of his assertion that the believer dies with Christ. It is only because it is the effect of Christ's cross to destroy the old dominion and the corporate "old man," and so put to death the many whose existence is bound up with these entities, that there is any possibility of this death to the old dominion being realized in the lives of particular individuals through baptism and faith[104]. Since the transfer from the old dominion to the new which takes place through dying with Christ is the effect of Christ's death, we must recognize that Paul, in speaking of dying with Christ, is referring primarily to the significance of Christ's death for men. This will become clearer as we note that in other passages Paul, on the one hand, makes no mention of baptism, and on the other, indicates that he is speaking directly of the significance of Christ's cross.

It must now be shown that the interpretation of Rom. 6 advanced in this section is supported by other passages in which Paul uses the motif of dying and rising with Christ[105].

2. Romans 7 1-6

In the basic pattern of thought, Rom. 7 1-6 continues Rom. 6. Just as the preceding chapter, Rom. 7 1-6 refers to a bondage, release from this bondage, and entry into a new bondage, and just as there it is through dying with Christ that this decisive transition takes place. A number of the same concepts are used. Καταργέω is used in 6 6, 7 2 and 7 6 to describe the end of the old bondage. The old and new bondages are described with the words κυριεύω in 6 9, 14, and 7 1, and δουλεύω or δοῦλος in 6 6, 16ff., and 7 6. We find the same use of the dative to indicate the lord to whom one lives or dies in 7 4 as in 6 2, 10-11. Finally, the idea of having or bearing fruit carries over from 6 21-22 to 7 4-5. However, there is also a significant change from Rom. 6, for now it is the law rather than sin to which the believers die. To be sure, the law is never far from Paul's mind in Romans and is mentioned even in Rom. 6 (vss. 14-15). Rom. 7 1-6 reaches back to these verses, and beyond them to 5 20, and in so doing prepares the way for the discussion of the law which will follow in the rest of chapter 7. Thus this section belongs both to what pre-

---

[104] Why Christ's cross has this effect will be more fully explained on pp. 123—27.
[105] On Rom. 6 see further pp. 77—83, where the relation of dying and rising with Christ to Paul's ethical imperative is discussed.

cedes and what follows, the train of thought being woven like a rope rather than sharply divided into sections. With respect to the ideas of the two bondages and dying with Christ, Rom. 7 1-6 continues the thought of chapter 6. With respect to the question which is treated in these terms, that of the law, it begins the discussion which follows.

Along with the problem of the law Paul brings in new variations on the idea of bondage. He begins with a maxim: "The law exercises lordship over a man for as long as he lives."[1] Then he takes up an example from the law itself, that of the legal bondage of the wife to her husband during his lifetime and her release from this bondage in the case of his death. In bringing in this new variation on the same basic idea, Paul also uses some new constructions. He speaks of being "bound by law," using the verb δέω, and uses a construction with γίνομαι and dative in vss. 3-4, meaning "to belong to." This is based on a classical Greek construction, but is probably influenced here by its use in the Old Testament in connection with marriage[2]. This indicates, of course, the joining of man and woman in the marriage relationship, but not as equal partners, for the man is the woman's master. Vss. 5-6 contrast the two dominions in terms of "flesh" and "oldness of letter," on the one hand, and "newness of Spirit," on the other. These terms are very important for Paul's discussion of the two dominions in the passages which follow in Romans[3].

It has been frequently noted that the maxim of vs. 1, in which release from the law is through a person's own death, does not fit with the illustration from marriage law in vss. 2-3, where the wife is released by the *husband's* death, nor this with vs. 4, in which it is stated that "*you* have been put to death." It is sometimes concluded from this that the only point of comparison is the general idea of freedom through a death[4], but actually *both* the maxim of vs. 1 and the illustration of vss. 2-3 correspond in detail to what happens to the Christian. The statement in vs. 4 that the believers have been "put to death" agrees with vs. 1, where release from the law comes through a person's own death. On the other hand, vs. 4 also continues the thought of vss. 2-3. Just as death releases a wife so that she may belong to another husband, so the believers "belong to another, to the one who was raised from the dead."[5] The fact

---

[1] Cp. 6 7.   [2] Cf. LXX Lev. 22 12 and BLASS-DEBRUNNER, sect. 189.

[3] Cf. especially 8 2ff.

[4] So Kuss, Römerbrief, p. 436.

[5] This reference to Christ's resurrection, which is not developed here, shows the tendency of the passages which use the motif we are examining to refer both to death and to resurrection.

2. Romans 7 1-6

that both ideas, that the Christians die (vs. 1) and that they live on and belong to a new husband (vss. 2-3), are combined in vs. 4 shows the reason for the confusion here. No example will quite fit what Paul wishes to say, for the Christians are both the ones who die and the ones who live on under a new master[6]. Dying with Christ is something more than a figure of speech which can be changed to fit Paul's illustrations. Instead, Paul uses two different ideas to illustrate what he wishes to say about dying with Christ to the law.

Vs. 4 makes no use of the preposition σύν. Nevertheless, it refers to the death of the believers and, as we will see below, connects this to the death of Christ. If further proof is needed that we have here the motif of dying with Christ, it is supplied by Gal. 2 19, where "I died to the law" is followed by Χριστῷ συνεσταύρωμαι. The passive ἐθανατώθητε in Rom. 7 4 shows that this death is not primarily a matter of a human act, for instance, in imitating Christ, but of God's action upon men. This emphasis on what has happened to the believers, rather than on their own act, is typical of the passages discussed in Part I, Gal. 5 24 being the only clear exception. The phrase "through the body of Christ" has caused the exegetes considerable difficulty. At first glance there seem to be two possibilities of interpretation: either to understand "the body of Christ" as the body of Jesus which hung on the cross, or to understand it as referring to the church, as in Rom. 12 5 and I Cor. 12 12ff. However, neither of these interpretations is adequate. To simply say that Rom. 7 4 refers to the physical body of Jesus on the cross is inadequate, for this does not explain the fact that *"you* were put to death" through this body. The believers themselves have been put to death through the body of Christ. Since the body of Christ must be understood in a way which explains this fact, it is natural to refer to Rom. 12 5 and I Cor. 12 12ff., where this phrase has a corporate sense. However, this does not solve the problem either. That Paul uses the phrase "body of Christ" in a corporate sense is an important fact, but it is misleading to simply interpret Rom. 7 4 on the basis of Rom. 12 5 and I Cor. 12 12ff. In these passages the phrase has a different function in Paul's thought, namely, to bring out the relation of members to the whole. Nothing is said about the dying of this body. However, in Rom. 7 4 the "body of Christ" is the means by which the believers were put to death. No other function of this body is mentioned. The church as the body of Christ could hardly be more than a remote cause of the believers' death in Paul's mind. Rather, we would expect some reference to Jesus' crucifixion, for passages which are closely related to Rom. 7 1-6, such as Rom. 6 and

---

[6] So PAUL ALTHAUS, Der Brief an die Römer, 9. Aufl. Göttingen 1959, p. 64.

Gal. 2 19-20, bring out the connection between the death of the believer to the old bondage and the death of Jesus. The believers die only because they die with Christ. In order to explain how the believers die through this body it seems necessary to assert that the "body of Christ" is both the physical body of Christ which died on the cross and a corporate body in which the believers are present.

How are we to understand this? It is not sufficient to assert the unity of the one body of Christ in its different manifestations, so that Paul can easily move from the physical body to the church as the body of Christ[7]. This both ignores the difference between the use of "body of Christ" here and in Rom. 12 5 and I Cor. 12 12ff., and overlooks some much closer parallels to Rom. 7 4. In two other passages which speak of dying and rising with Christ we find reference to a collective "body" which dies in that Christ dies. The first of these is Rom. 6 6. There we find reference to the destruction of "the body of sin," and this is closely paralleled by the crucifixion of "our old man" with Christ. In discussing this verse it was shown that this "old man" was a corporate entity[8]. Therefore, the parallel phrase "body of sin" must be understood in the same way. This fits the argument of the passage, for the destruction of the "body of sin" means that the believers are no longer slaves to sin. But this is so because the believers have themselves died to sin (cf. Rom. 6 7). As has been shown, this does not mean that each believer has died separately, but that all have died in Christ's death. This must be the meaning of the destruction of the body of sin also. It was also pointed out above that the crucifixion of the "old man" with Christ implies that Christ was himself the bearer of this collective reality of the old aeon[9]. Therefore, it is not so strange as it might at first appear that Paul should refer in Rom. 6 6 to the "body of sin" and in Rom. 7 4 to the "body of Christ," yet mean the same thing. The second parallel verse is Col. 2 11. There in a closely related setting the author refers to "the stripping off of the body of the flesh." When this verse is discussed, it will be shown that it also refers to Christ's death as an event in which the believers participate[10]. These closely related passages show that the "body of Christ" in Rom. 7 4 refers not to the church, the collective body of the new aeon, but to the collective body of the old aeon, the body of "sin" or "flesh." The believers

---

[7] So TRAUGOTT SCHMIDT, Der Leib Christi, pp. 213—17, and, more recently, some English scholars: L. S. THORNTON, The Common Life in the Body of Christ, 2nd Ed. Westminster 1944, *passim*; J. A. T. ROBINSON, The Body: A Study in Pauline Theology, London 1952, pp. 47—46.
[8] Cf. pp. 25—27.
[9] Cf. pp. 27—28.
[10] Cf. pp. 48—50.

were put to death through this body because this body was put to death in the crucifixion of Christ and the believers were included in it.

Paul does not mention baptism in these verses. Indeed, it is clear that he is speaking directly of what took place through the body of Christ which was nailed to the cross. Thus the fact that the believer shares in Christ's death is not first made possible by a special power in the sacrament. Rather, the believer's participation in the cross is based upon the fact that the cross is itself an eschatological and inclusive event. Baptism has a role in the concrete realization of dying with Christ in the life of the individual, for in baptism the power of the cross as eschatological event is manifest, but baptism does not first give to Christ's cross its character as inclusive event by repeating this event or making it present as it otherwise could not be present.

3. Ephesians and Colossians

For the purposes of this study passages from Ephesians and Colossians can only have a supplementary role. The question of the authorship of these two writings is complex and cannot be discussed here. It is clear, however, that we cannot simply presuppose that these are the writings of Paul. Since the focus of attention of this study is *Paul's* use of the motif of dying and rising with Christ, we must rely for evidence primarily on the seven letters which are most widely recognized as written by Paul. Features of this motif which do not occur in these seven letters cannot with any certainty be ascribed to Paul and cannot serve as a basis for the interpretation of Paul's usage in general. There are some unusual features of this motif in Ephesians and Colossians. It has often been noted that only in Ephesians and Colossians is rising with Christ referred to as a past event. In the Pauline homologoumena the believer's participation in Christ's resurrection is spoken of either as still future or as present in the midst of temptation and suffering. It has already been shown that this difference touches an issue of considerable importance to Paul[1]. Therefore, it cannot be explained as a merely stylistic variation or as caused by the differing situations of the different letters. The believers' past resurrection with Christ plays an important role in the thought of Ephesians and Colossians. In Colossians the imperative is based not only on the past death with Christ, but also on this past resurrection (3 1). This is accompanied by the idea that

---

[1] Cf. pp. 10—12.

"things above," rather than earthly things, are the proper concern of the Christian. This implies that the life of the believer is already a heavenly life, even though it is still hidden (3 3). The connection between this past resurrection with Christ and heavenly exaltation is even clearer in Eph. 2 6, where the motif of dying and rising with Christ is expanded to include being seated with Christ in the heavenly places. In this passage the saving event is reduced to this resurrection and exaltation with Christ alone, for there is no mention of dying with Christ. Instead, the previous life of the believer is spoken of as a state of deadness (2 1, 5). Thus, it is not asserted that the believer participates in Christ's death. Passages in the Pauline homologoumena which use the motif of dying and rising with Christ with reference to the past always speak of dying as an event, and this is connected with the event of Christ's cross. The state previous to this is not described as deadness but as a life of a different kind (II Cor. 5 15, Gal. 2 20; cf. Rom. 6 2). Reference to a state of deadness is found in Col. 2 13 also, though in Colossians this alternates with the idea of dying with Christ (2 20, 3 3). In speaking of dying with Christ Col. 2 20 exhibits an unusual stylistic feature, for it uses the preposition ἀπό where Pauline style would lead us to expect a simple dative[2].

Although the significance of the motif of dying and rising with Christ in Ephesians and Colossians cannot be discussed in full here, there is one passage in these letters which is able to supplement the argument of this study. Col. 2—3 provides additional evidence that the motif of dying and rising with Christ is connected to the idea of an inclusive body and an inclusive man. This material may be used as evidence for this connection without arguing that Colossians was written by Paul. This connection has already been shown to be present in the letter to the Romans. Colossians, even if not written by Paul, clearly stands in the Pauline tradition and reflects patterns of thought used by Paul. Colossians may even bring out more clearly certain ideas which are only touched upon in the Pauline homologoumena. Paul worked with the tradition of the Hellenistic church of which he was a part. Colossians reflects this same tradition, and is able to clarify some of the ideas which Paul refers to, but does not explain. Such is the case with Paul's reference to "our old man" in Rom. 6 6, for instance. Therefore, it is worth our while to consider the connection between dying and rising with Christ and ideas of an inclusive body and man which we find in Col. 2—3.

Col. 2 9ff. has a hymnlike structure, basic to which is the repeated ἐν αὐτῷ or ἐν ᾧ. Within this structure is brought out the believers' participation in Christ's fullness, death, burial, and resur-

---

[2] Cf. p. 18.

rection. In vss. 12-13 this is developed in familiar terms through verbs compounded with συν-. However, the idea of the believers' participation in all that Christ is and did is apparent from vs. 10 on. Thus the letter first declares that the whole fullness of divinity dwells in Christ, and then adds, "You have come to fullness in him." This "in him" is picked up at the beginning of vs. 11 by ἐν ᾧ: ". . . in whom also you were circumcised with a circumcision not made with hands in the stripping off of the body of the flesh, in the circumcision of Christ . . ."[3]. "Circumcision" and "stripping off the body of the flesh" may reflect ideas connected with baptism, which is mentioned in the next verse. However, the fact that the believers were circumcised *in Christ* shows that the thought here is not restricted to what happened to the believers any more than it is in the rest of this section. Rather, the believers were circumcised in the stripping off of the body of the flesh because Christ was so circumcised and the believers participated in this. Thus this is "the circumcision of Christ" because it is the circumcision which Christ underwent. This verse, then, refers to the crucifixion of Christ, just as the following verse refers to his burial and resurrection. It is in his crucifixion that this "stripping off of the body of the flesh" took place. This "body of the flesh" corresponds to "the body of sin" in Rom. 6 6 and to "the body of Christ" in Rom. 7 4. Just as in Romans this body is an inclusive body, for "in him" the believers were also "circumcised . . . in the stripping off of the body of the flesh." We have here, then, a parallel to Rom. 6 6 and 7 4, showing the same features of a corporate body of the old aeon which in the crucifixion of Christ is destroyed, and so the old life of the believers with it. In the sequence of death-burial-resurrection which we find in vss. 11-12, vs. 11 refers to the crucifixion, thereby taking the place of an explicit use of συσταυρόω or some similar verb which would conform with the συν- verbs which follow. Thus we see that the ideas of the destruction of a collective entity through Christ's death and of dying and rising with Christ not only occur together, but are interchangeable, and so must have the same meaning.

We have now found clear indication in three passages, Rom. 6 6, 7 4, and Col. 2 11, of an identification of Christ's body on the cross with the inclusive body of the old aeon. According to Col. 2 11 this body is stripped off. Since this takes place through the physical death of

---

[3] ERNST LOHMEYER connects this last phrase with the following so as to show three strophes, each with three members, beginning with ἐν ᾧ vs. 11, ἐν τῇ περιτομῇ vs. 11, and ἐν ᾧ vs. 12, and referring first to the crucifixion, then the burial, then the resurrection of Christ, and the believers with him. Die Briefe an die Philipper, an die Kolosser und an Philemon, 10. Aufl. Göttingen 1954, pp. 101—02. This is possible, but it is not obvious that ἐν τῇ περιτομῇ τοῦ Χριστοῦ begins a new strophe.

Christ, this body must be the physical body which Christ "wore."[4] We have here a view of Christ as a redeemer who redeems *in that* he strips off the body of flesh, conceived as something negative. This means redemption because this "body of the flesh" is something foreign to his true existence and to that of the many who are included in him. Presumably, that which is left over after this body is stripped off is what is redeemed from this evil state. This conception seems to have its background in a dualistic mythology. It is not fully developed in Col. 2 11, and even less so in Rom. 6 6 and 7 4, probably because the full implications of this pattern of thought were unacceptable. However, in one respect this conception was useful to Paul. It conceived Christ's death as an inclusive event, and so as the means by which the believers have died to the old dominion.

In Rom. 6 6 the destruction of the body of sin is paralleled by the crucifixion of "our old man." In Colossians also dying with Christ is connected not only with the stripping off of a body but also with the stripping off of the old man (3 9). The close connection of 3 9 with 2 11 is shown by the reoccurrence of the unusual idea of "stripping off."[5] This would suggest that stripping off the old man also has some connection to dying with Christ. And there is additional evidence for such a connection.

In Col. 3 9-10 stripping off the old man is contrasted with putting on the new man. This old man and new man are corporate figures, as has been shown[6]. These ideas are introduced at this point in order to support the author's exhortation. The idea of putting on the new man is continued by the imperative of the same verb in vs. 12. But there, instead of the new man, it is a series of five virtues which are to be "put on." There must be a close relation between the new man and these virtues. There is a similar relation between the old man and certain vices. Vs. 9 speaks of stripping off the old man "with his deeds." These "deeds" of the old man evidently refer to the two lists of vices in vss. 5 and 8. The connection between the old man and these vices is expressed in another way in vs. 5. There the list of vices stands in apposition to τὰ μέλη τὰ ἐπὶ τῆς γῆς. These vices are here understood as the "members" of the old man. The close connection pointed out above between the two inclusive men and lists of vices and virtues supports this. Other interpretations have serious faults. To understand τὰ μέλη as the members of each individual's body would damage the argument of the letter. The fact

---

[4] Ἀπέκδυσις plays upon the idea of taking off a garment.

[5] Ἀπεκδύομαι and ἀπέκδυσις occur only in these two chapters in the New Testament. Ἀπέκδυσις occurs nowhere else independently of Col. 2 11. Cf. BAUER (A—G), *sub verbo*.

[6] Cf. p. 25.

that the vices stand in apposition to τὰ μέλη shows that speaking of the members of the individual's body, when wrongly used, as a basis for the vices is a false weakening of the meaning. Rather, the "members" are themselves the vices. If this is applied to the members of the individual's body, it contrasts strangely with what has just been said against the asceticism of the opponents in Colossae. CHARLES MASSON, seeing this difficulty, explains τὰ μέλη as a vocative[7]. The believers are being addressed as members of the body of Christ. But this is a strained interpretation. The mention of the church as a body in 2 19 is too far away, and the word order, with immediate repetition of the article τὰ, most naturally indicates the connection of τὰ μέλη with what follows[8]. Indeed, one of MASSON's main arguments is that no other interpretation makes sense in the context, but he failed to consider the interpretation given above, that the "members" are the members of the old man.

This conception is not without parallel. We have already seen that the ideas of an inclusive man and an inclusive body occur together in Rom. 6 6 and have noted a connection between these ideas in Col. 2 11 and 3 9. This connection could easily lead to discussion of the "members" of the old man. The fact that the members of this man or body are vices, or, in the case of the new man, virtues, has parallels in Hellenistic literature. Corpus Hermeticum XIII, 7—9 speaks of the body of the reborn man, who is cosmic in scope, penetrating all things, as consisting of divine powers or virtues. Related ideas seem to be present in the writings of Philo of Alexandria. In De Fuga et Inventione 110 and 112 Philo discusses the high priest and his garments, giving a triple interpretation in terms of relations which he sees as parallel: the Logos and the cosmos, "the soul in the partial sense" and the body, and the mind and the virtues. In each case the former puts on the latter as garments. We find references elsewhere in Philo to the body as clothing which is put on[9] and to the world as body of the Logos[10]. The parallel here between the cosmos, the physical body, and the virtues, each of which is "put on," suggests that they are all thought of as the "body" of that which clothes itself in them. In that case, we have in this one passage reference both to the virtues as the body of the mind and to the cosmos as the body of the Logos. The Logos is elsewhere given the title *anthropos*[11]. We see, then, that the reference in Col. 3 5ff. to an in-

---

[7] L'épître de saint Paul aux Colossiens, Neuchâtel 1950, p. 142.
[8] Τὰ ἐπὶ τῆς γῆς must refer to the vices. Cf. 3 2.
[9] Cf. Quaest in Gn I, 53.
[10] Cf. Quaest in Ex II, 117.
[11] Conf Ling 41, 62, 146.

clusive man whose members are virtues or vices does not occur in a vacuum[12].

This interpretation of Col. 3 5 is important because it shows that the ideas of dying with Christ and of the death of the old man come together in this verse. Col. 3 5ff. is part of a longer argument which contrasts the demands of the opponents, which are described as the commandments of *men*, with the new ethical life demanded of Christians on the basis of their new existence. From 2 20 to 3 5 this is developed in terms of dying and rising with Christ. This motif is used as the basis for the exhortation. It is the indicative from which the imperative is drawn, as we see in 3 1. Similarly, 3 5 is the imperative drawn from the indicative of 3 3, and this imperative is expressed in language which continues the thought of dying with Christ (νεκρώσατε)[13]. Now it is the *members of the old man* which must be put to death. Here we find one more instance of the connection between dying with Christ and the death of the inclusive reality of the old aeon. Thus it is not surprising that in vss. 9-10 the reference to stripping off the old and putting on the new man plays the same role in the argument as dying and rising with Christ in the preceding verses, that of the indicative which forms the basis of the imperative[14], and that vss. 5 and 12, which show parallel form, are formulated one with νεκρώσατε and the other with ἐνδύσασθε. The ideas of dying and rising with Christ and of stripping off the old man and putting on the new man have, in fact, the same significance for the author.

Rom. 6 6, 7 4 and Col. 2 11-12, 3 5ff. provide the principal evidence for the assertion that in speaking of dying with Christ Paul understands Christ's death as an inclusive event in which a corporate entity was put to death. However, we will see that not only in Romans, but also in other places, especially Gal. 2 19 and 6 14, Paul is speaking directly of what has taken place in Christ's cross when referring to dying with Christ. That Paul understands Christ's cross as an inclusive event explains this fact.

It is also possible to show why it was natural for Paul to connect the motif of dying and rising with Christ to the idea of an inclusive man. Both of these patterns of thought were connected at an early date with Christian baptism. Therefore, even if they were originally

---

[12] See further ERNST KÄSEMANN, Leib und Leib Christi, Tübingen 1933, pp. 59—65, 74—80, 85f., 150; and RICHARD REITZENSTEIN, Die hellenistischen Mysterienreligionen, 3. Aufl. Stuttgart 1956, pp. 265—275, and Das iranische Erlösungsmysterium, Bonn 1921, pp. 152—163.

[13] Cp. Rom. 8 13, which is discussed on pp. 79—80.

[14] The participles ἀπεκδυσάμενοι and ἐνδυσάμενοι are to be understood in a causal, not an imperative sense. Cf. MASSON, Colossiens, p. 143, n. 6, and JACOB JERVELL, Imago Dei, Göttingen 1960, pp. 235—36.

separate, a connection between them would have quickly developed in Christian thought. To be sure, Paul gives the motif of dying and rising with Christ an important function within his theology as a whole, rather than using it primarily to interpret the sacrament of baptism. However, Rom. 6 and Col. 2 12 make clear that this motif did have a connection with baptism, and it has been shown that this connection reflects a tradition known beyond Pauline circles[15]. The fact that Paul in Rom. 6 6 refers at the same time to the crucifixion of "our old man" without explaining this phrase probably indicates that this idea was already part of the tradition. In any case, the idea of an inclusive man is clearly connected with baptism in Paul's letters. It has already been shown that the idea of baptism "into Christ" refers to entry into Christ as the inclusive figure of the new aeon[16]. This phrase is important for Paul's understanding of baptism, for apart from two passages which deal with special problems[17], every passage in the Pauline homologoumena which explicitly uses the terms βαπτίζω and βάπτισμα employs this or an analogous construction[18]. In Gal. 3 27-28 the connection of this construction with the idea of Christ as an inclusive person is especially clear.

The references to the old man and the new man in Col. 3 9-11 also have a background in baptismal patterns of thought. This is shown by the following considerations: 1) This passage is closely related to Gal. 3 27-28 through the idea of "putting on" an inclusive man and through the motif of the overcoming of the divisions of the old world (Col. 3 11). That Col. 3 11 reflects a set pattern of thought which is connected with baptism is shown not only by Gal. 3 28, but also by I Cor. 12 13. 2) The baptismal background of this passage is clear from the development of the exhortation from 2 20 on in terms of dying and rising with Christ. This theme not only occurs next to that of the old man and new man, but is intermingled with it[19]. 3) In the preceding chapter (2 11-12) dying and rising with Christ is also combined with the idea of an inclusive figure[20], and there we find explicit reference to baptism. The connection of these two passages is shown by the use of the rare words ἀπεκδύομαι and ἀπέκδυσις[21]. 4) PHILIP CARRINGTON has shown that the verb ἀποτίθημι in 3 8 is characteristic of a widespread catechetical pattern[22]. The

---

[15] Cf. pp. 7—14.   [16] Cf. pp. 22—24.
[17] I Cor. 1 13-17, 15 29.
[18] I. e., εἰς τὸν θάνατον — Rom. 6 3-4; εἰς τὸν Μωϋσῆν — I Cor. 10 2; εἰς ἓν σῶμα — I Cor. 12 13.   [19] 3 5. Cf. above, pp. 50—52.
[20] Cf. above, pp. 48—50.   [21] Cf. p. 50, n. 5.
[22] The Primitive Christian Catechism, Cambridge 1940, pp. 46—49. To what extent the complete pattern which CARRINGTON works out is to be accepted does not concern us here.

connection of this catechetical material with baptism is shown by the fact that in four passages in which this verb is used in exhortation (Col. 3 8; Eph. 4 22, 25; I Peter 2 1; James 1 21) it is related to the fact of new creation or new birth (Col. 3 10; Eph. 4 24; I Peter 1 23, 2 2; James 1 18)[23]. This is striking since the verb occurs in exhortation in only two other passages, Hebrews 12 1 and Rom. 13 12[24]. 5) The contrast between old man and new man fits in well with the transition which took place in baptism. This evidence shows that Col. 3 9-10 makes use of baptismal ideas. The same must be said for the same ideas in Eph. 4 22-24 and 2 15[25], and also in Rom. 6 6. Since they were both used in connection with baptism, it is not surprising that the ideas of dying and rising with Christ and of stripping off the old inclusive man and putting on the new were brought together at an early period, and so it should not be surprising that Paul relates dying and rising with Christ to such inclusive patterns of thought.

The connection of these ideas with baptism illumines one further point which is important in Paul's use of dying and rising with Christ. Baptism seems to have been understood at an early date as a change of lordship, a freeing of the one baptized from hostile powers and a transfer to the protection of the Lord Jesus. Col. 1 12-14 refers to such a transfer in language which probably reflects baptismal tradition[26]. We have already seen that Paul refers to baptism in Rom. 6 because he is interested in this transfer from one lord to another, and we will see that this idea is a constant feature of those passages which refer to dying with Christ as a past event. The complex of thought which we find in these passages was a natural one for Paul. The major elements of this complex of thought, that is, the ideas of transfer from one lordship to another, of dying and rising with Christ, and of an inclusive person, were already related through a common connection with baptism. Paul takes up this complex of ideas, deepens and broadens it, and uses it to express fundamental aspects of his understanding of the cross, the resurrection, and the new existence based on these events.

---

[23] For an extensive argument that new creation after the image of God is connected with baptism see JACOB JERVELL, Imago Dei, pp. 197 ff., 231 ff.

[24] It occurs in other senses at Mat. 14 8 and Acts 7 58. Rom. 13 12 may also be connected with baptism. Cp. vs. 14 with Gal. 3 27.

[25] Note here also the emphasis on new creation and the new unity.

[26] Cf. ERNST KÄSEMANN, "Eine urchristliche Tauflikurgie," Exegetische Versuche, vol. 1, pp. 37—39, 43—47.

4. Galatians 2 19-20

In order to understand the significance of these verses for Paul, we must, of course, understand them in their context. This presents us with a problem, for interpreters are not agreed on how to relate these verses to Paul's preceding argument. In vs. 17 Paul raises the question of whether Christ is a servant of sin[1]. This is promptly denied. One would expect argument supporting this denial to follow. Since vss. 18 and 19 are connected to the preceding by γάρ, they seem to be intended to provide this support[2]. An interpretation which is able to make clear a progress in the thought corresponding to these connectives is to be preferred. In vs. 17 the emphatic εὑρέθημεν καὶ αὐτοὶ ἁμαρτωλοί is surely meant to refer to Paul, and to those who stand with him in some respect. But how is it that Paul and these others were "found sinners"? There is no justification for reading this sentence as a condition contrary to fact, for, while we do encounter such conditions without the particle ἄν[3], it would be necessary here either to use this particle or a verb in augment tense in the apodosis. Otherwise the reader will most naturally supply a present verb in the apodosis and interpret the whole sentence as a reference to reality. Vs. 17, then, cannot be merely hypothetical, but must refer to a serious accusation against Paul. Paul and those with him must have actually been "found sinners" in someone's eyes[4]. HEINRICH SCHLIER, noting this, understands the "we" as Paul and the other Jewish Christians and refers being "found sinners" to the event of their conversion[5]. Admitting that they also were sinners, even though this put them on the same level with the gentiles, was the precondition for "seeking to be justified in Christ." The objection, according to SCHLIER, rests upon the fact that Christ has justified

---
[1] We should read ἆρα, not ἄρα, and understand what follows as a rhetorical question. Paul regularly uses μὴ γένοιτο to negate such a question, and understanding vs. 17 in this way results in a smoother train of thought.

[2] ALBRECHT OEPKE says, "Die Aussage [vs. 19] eignet sich weder zur Begründung von vs. 18 noch von vs. 17c. Wir haben daher hier einen der seltenen Fälle, wo γάρ nicht Vorhergehendes begründet, sondern metabatisch die Wichtigkeit des Folgenden unterstreicht: 'Ich nun...'" Der Brief des Paulus an die Galater, 2. Aufl. Berlin 1957, p. 62. This could only be accepted as a last resort, not only because this usage is unusual, but because then the denial of the charge in vs. 17 is only supported by the *ad hominem* argument in vs. 18, and vs. 19 is left without a real connection with the preceding verses.

[3] Cf. BLASS-DEBRUNNER, sect. 360, 1.

[4] As BLASS-DEBRUNNER, sect. 371—72, point out, this conditional construction is used in the New Testament, with very few exceptions, of conditions which are regarded as, or asserted to be, fulfilled.

[5] Der Brief an die Galater, 11. Aufl. Göttingen 1951, pp. 58—59.

such sinners, and is comparable to the charge of the Pharisees against Jesus that he received sinners[6]. But can this accusation be explained merely from the fact that they had previously been sinners and yet were accepted by Christ? I think not, for this in itself would not make Christ a servant of sin in the eyes of the opponents. Judaism was acquainted with repentance. The repentant sinner could be accepted so long as *from now on* he would live by the law. The assertion that Christ is made a servant of sin must rest on some other basis than the fact that Christ accepts those who were sinners but have decided to do better. That this does, indeed, refer to something else is shown by the present participle ζητοῦντες. It is true, as SCHLIER points out, that "seeking to be justified in Christ" is not to be distinguished from faith[7], but the continuative present participle is not equivalent to the aorist ἐπιστεύσαμεν in vs. 16, but refers to the life of faith which Paul, and those with him, have been leading[8]. Accompanied by this present participle, the aorist εὑρέθημεν can only refer to Paul's life as a Christian. The punctiliar character of the aorist suggests that Paul has a particular event in mind. This is probably the difficulty in Antioch mentioned in vss. 11-14. Ἁμαρτωλοί, then, is used in vs. 17 in the same sense as in vs. 15. Paul was a sinner in the judgment of the Jewish law, which necessarily places all gentiles in this class, and also any Jew who does not keep the food laws. At Antioch Paul was found to be a sinner in the eyes of his opponents. Moreover, he was found to be a sinner in the eyes of the law, according to which his opponents judged. It is important to see that there is no distinction in vs. 17 or in what follows between "ritual" and "ethical" commandments. For the Jew, and for Paul, the law is valid because it is commanded by God, and if one has transgressed any commandment, he is a sinner. The charge of the opponents referred to in vs. 17 has some plausibility. Paul had, indeed, transgressed the law and by his action and teaching made Christ a servant of sin — if the law is still in force for the Christian.

It is this presupposition of the charge which Paul denies. First of all he brings in an *ad hominem* argument to support his denial of the charge. It is not in what Paul has done, but in building up the law after having torn it down that one proves himself a transgressor. Behind the "I" stands not Paul himself but Peter and the others mentioned in vss. 11-13. In vs. 18 it is clearly a question of trans-

---

[6] *Ibid.*, p. 59.

[7] *Ibid.*, p. 58, n. 7.

[8] Cf. PIERRE BONNARD, L'épître de saint Paul aux Galates, Neuchâtel 1953, p. 54. That Paul can speak of *Christian* existence as *seeking* to be justified is not surprising, since justification for Paul continues to have a connection with one's standing before God in the last judgment. Cp. Gal. 5 5: "hope of justification."

4. Galatians 2 19-20

gression of the law, and of whether the law is still in force, i. e., of whether it is "torn down" or "built up." This supports what was said regarding vs. 17 and points to the connection between vs. 17 and vss. 19-20. Vss. 19-20 give Paul's basic answer to the charge. It does not hold because Paul has died to the law through crucifixion with Christ. He no longer lives under the law's power. This interpretation makes the progress of Paul's thought in vss. 17-19 clear. In particular, it shows why Paul answers the charge of being found a sinner and making Christ a servant of sin by asserting that he has died to the *law*, and not to sin.

Paul refers here to dying with Christ because it is necessary for him to emphasize his radical break with the old life under the law, and the newness of Christian existence. The law's condemnation is real, but it is a reality of the old dominion[9]. The Christian has died with Christ to this old dominion of the law, and it is because of this, and this alone, that he is now free from the law's condemnation and participates in a *new* life, one which is neither a life of "works of the law" nor the sinful life of the lawbreaker, but a new life "to God," of Christ living "in me."

In vss. 19-20 Paul speaks in the first person singular. This is not because he is referring to a personal, perhaps mystical, experience. We have already seen from our study of Rom. 7 4 that what Paul is talking about here is not his own private experience, but something which is valid for every Christian. The first person singular is used here because this is part of Paul's defense of his own conduct. The emphatic ἐγώ appears in vs. 19 because of the contrast with the "I" of vs. 18, which refers to the Christian who falls back into dependence upon the law. The ἐγώ in vs. 20 is caused by the contrast with Χριστός. Since this verse refers to the new life which is the result of dying with Christ, it can no more be limited to Paul's personal experience than dying with Christ can[10].

The false subjectivizing which shows itself in the attempt to refer these verses to a personal experience of Paul is also to be guarded against in the interpretation of διὰ νόμου in vs. 19. We are pointed in the right direction when we see that vs. 19 shows the same construction with the dative that we met in Rom. 6 2, 10-11 and 7 4. Previously it was indicated that this construction is used in connection with one's release from one lordship and entry into another, the dative indicating the lord in question[11]. As we have seen, each of the two lords is a slave master who holds men in bondage. A man is

---

[9] Cf. Rom. 7 6, Gal. 3 22—4 5.
[10] On vs. 20 see below, pp. 59—61.
[11] Cf. p. 18.

determined by the power sphere within which he exists, and a change can only take place if the powers which enslave a man change[12]. This is not something which happens primarily in the individual's mind, but a matter of an eschatological change through God's action. Therefore, we cannot explain the function of the law (διὰ νόμου) in dying to the law by interpretations which speak only of the individual's consciousness. It is not a matter of the law bringing men to a realization of their sin before the law. Nor is it a matter of the individual gaining insight through the law that the law is not able to justify. The law is a power of the old aeon, closely connected to sin and death, and one cannot die to it merely by being conscious of one's bondage. There are other interpretations which must be rejected also. Διὰ νόμου does not refer to the Old Testament as a whole, which, in its positive function of announcing Christ, puts an end to itself, nor to the law of Christ in contrast to the Jewish law. Neither of these interpretations is justified by the context, for here Paul is speaking only of the law as the commandments which his opponents insist must be obeyed and before which Paul and his followers were "found sinners."

There is evidence which points to a different interpretation of διὰ νόμου. Besides mentioning that this death was "through law," Paul gives one other indication of how his death to law took place. In vs. 19b he rephrases his statement to bring out the connection of this death to the crucifixion of Christ: "I have been crucified with Christ." Since dying to the law takes place through crucifixion with Christ, it is well to consider the function of the law in the crucifixion of *Christ* before attempting to explain the phrase διὰ νόμου. Paul discusses the relation of Christ to the law in the following chapters of Galatians. In 3 13 he asserts that the law played a role in Christ's death. Christ died under the curse of the law. He bore its full condemnation in his death, "having become a curse for us," but he thereby "ransomed us from the curse of the law." Because the law plays a role in Christ's death, it is also indirectly instrumental in the ransom of the believers from its own curse. For Paul this ransom not only means release from guilt before the law; it also means release from its power and demand, the kind of release which is referred to when Paul speaks of dying to the law. This is shown by Gal. 4 3-5, which also speaks of Christ's subjection to the law and the ransom of the believers which results from this. In 3 22—4 5 it is clear that the law was a confining and enslaving power, and that the ransom of the believers meant release from this slavery. These references to Christ's subjection to law and endurance of its curse in his death

---

[12] Cf. pp. 70—72.

provide the background for a suitable understanding of the fact that Paul speaks of death to law as occurring "through law" in Gal. 2 19. The law indirectly has a role in the ransom of the believers from its own curse and slavery. This is because of its relation to *Christ*, not because of its effect on the individual Christian, for only through Christ does the curse and slavery of the law lead to ransom from the law. Thus the phrase διὰ νόμου in Gal. 2 19 is occasioned by the role of the law in Christ's death rather than by any effect which the law may have on the individual's consciousness. The believer's death to the law is also "through law" because he died in Christ's death. We see that here, just as in Rom. 6 6 and 7 4, Paul understands the believer to be directly included in Christ's crucifixion. It is the role of the law in this inclusive event which is referred to by διὰ νόμου.

The phrase "through law" also makes clear that Paul is not speaking of baptism in Gal. 2 19. This reference to the law can be understood only in connection with Christ's death under the law's curse on the cross. The law does not bring about a sacramental death in baptism.

Death to the law took place "in order that I might live to God." The nature of this new life is explained in vs. 20. It may be that in vs. 20 we have a form of speech derived from mystical ideas, but we must interpret this passage in the context of Paul's thought if we are to arrive at its meaning for Paul. It is clear that the idea of Christ living "in me" develops the thought of living "to God" in vs. 19 and refers to the new existence which stands in contrast to the old existence under the law. Just as the old existence is not based upon a mystical experience of the law or of the old dominion, so this new reality is not first of all a matter of the individual's subjective experience, but a new form of existence under a new power. Indeed, an appeal to mystical experience would be no reply to the charge raised in vs. 17, for freedom from the law can come only through God's eschatological act. Vs. 20a, then, is speaking of Christian existence in the new aeon, in which Christ has taken the place of the forces of the old aeon as the power at work in those of his dominion. This interpretation is supported by Paul's use of similar patterns of thought elsewhere. The assertion which is here made of Christ is made of *sin* in Rom. 7 17 and 20: "But now *I* am no longer producing it, but sin which is dwelling in me" (vs. 17). The "I" is replaced by the power at work in the dominion to which the self is in bondage. This power not only works from the outside, which would allow the self a certain independence, but dwells within and so exercises complete control. In Rom. 8 10 the idea of Christ being "in you" is used in a similar way. In this passage flesh and Spirit are contrasted as the two powers which determine those who are subject to them. One walks either "according to flesh" or "according to Spirit" (vs. 4). One exists either "in flesh" or "in Spirit" (vs. 9). In vs. 9 being "in Spirit" is connected with the indwelling of the Spirit of God and with having the Spirit of Christ. This indwelling of the Spirit is an essential part of what it means to belong to Christ (vs. 9b). It is not the private experience of certain individuals. Furthermore, this indwelling of the Spirit is equivalent to Christ being "in you" (vs. 10), which brings us to the formulation of Gal. 2 20. The changing terms "Spirit of God," "Spirit of Christ," and "Christ" indicate the one power which is active in the new aeon, dwelling in the believers and at work in them. The movement from one phrase to another shows that there is no sharp distinction between being "in Spirit," having the Spirit of God dwell "in you," having the "Spirit of Christ," and Christ being "in you." The reference to "Christ in you" is not a sudden jump from the idea of determination by an aeon power to mystical ideas. "Christ in you," in comparison to other formulations above, may express a greater concern with each individual's existence and action, but the basic idea of the determination of the life of the believer by the Master of the new dominion is the same. Gal. 2 20 is to be interpreted accordingly.

Vs. 20b has been interpreted as a qualification of the triumphant statement in vs. 20a. In other words, Paul is forced to concede that the present reality is only "faith" instead of this glorious, mystical "Christ in me."[13] This view has already been partially refuted. The refutation is complete when we consider the relation of this sentence to the rest of Paul's argument. The mystical interpretation of vss. 19-20 results in a very strange train of thought in this passage. In arguing for justification through faith in Christ instead of works of the law (vs. 16), Paul would suddenly jump out of context in vss. 19-20a to speak of his mystical experience, only to pull himself back to the lesser reality of faith in vs. 20b. However, we have seen that vss. 19-20a have a clear function in Paul's argument and are not a digression. Furthermore, there is no break between vss. 19-20a and vs. 20b, for vs. 20b simply develops the preceding thought by indicating that this new existence is existence in faith, which completes Paul's argument. By showing that the Christian has died to the law and now lives in faith Paul supports his basic assertion that the Christian is justified not from works of the law but from faith. If there is a concessive undertone in vs. 20b, it is in the reference to "what I now live in flesh," not in the reference to faith. In this initial clause it is admitted that the "I," which according to vs. 20a

---

[13] Cf. ERWIN WISSMANN, Das Verhältnis von ΠΙΣΤΙΣ und Christusfrömmigkeit bei Paulus, Göttingen 1926, p. 112.

no longer lives, does carry on a certain existence in the flesh even now. However, the sentence as a whole does not have this concessive sense, but asserts that this life in flesh has the positive quality of life in faith. The fact that ἐν πίστει is drawn forward as the first element of the main clause of the sentence, and the solemn, confessional elaboration of the object of this faith, help to make clear Paul's emphasis on this positive assertion.

This passage fits well with the other passages discussed in Part I. It speaks of the believers' release from the old dominion through Christ's death as an inclusive event, and of a new life to a new master. This new life is a life in faith, and one in which the concrete existence and action of the believer is determined by Christ, the Lord of the new dominion, living in him.

5. Galatians 5 24-25

These verses follow a rather extensive exhortation developed in terms of the two contrasting powers of flesh and Spirit. Flesh and Sqirit are active forces by which men walk (vss. 16, 25); they have desires (vss. 16-17); they oppose each other and prevent men from doing what they wish (vs. 17); they lead men (vs. 18), and have works (vs. 19), or fruit (vs. 22). We have here a version of the idea of the two dominions which emphasizes the activity of the two powers for the purpose of ethical exhortation. Vs. 24 brings in the indicative which belongs with the preceding imperative (vs. 16, cf. vs. 25). It speaks of the decisive, past event which is the basis of present existence and action.

Vss. 24-25 continue the contrast between flesh and Spirit, and the "flesh with the passions and the desires" is regarded as the object of crucifixion. That the power of the old aeon, rather than the believers, undergoes crucifixion is only a minor variation on what we have found in other passages, for in either case the same break with the old reality takes place[1]. However, the active form of the verb (ἐσταύρωσαν) is unusual. In this context Paul is evidently thinking of the believers' past decision which should form the basis of present action[2]. However, it is clear that men do not bring about this break

---

[1] Cf. Gal. 6 14, which asserts that "the world has been crucified to me and I to the world," using both formulations together.

[2] SCHLIER refers to baptism in connection with this verse. Cf. Galater, ad loc. Even if he is correct, the main emphasis is on the decision of faith connected with baptism rather than on what has happened to the believer through the sacrament. Against SCHLIER's view see BONNARD, Galates, p. 116. On the relation of faith to dying with Christ see pp. 123—26.

with the dominion of flesh on their own. The reference to crucifixion indicates the connection of this event with Christ's death, and the phrase οἱ . . . τοῦ Χριστοῦ indicates that this crucifixion is a reality within Christ's dominion. Furthermore, the way in which Paul speaks of dying with Christ in other passages, using passive formulations and referring to Christ's death as an inclusive event, makes clear that it is only through Christ's crucifixion that men are able to crucify the flesh.

Vs. 25 is not to be separated from vs. 24 as the beginning of a new section, for it completes vs. 24 with the reference to the new life which is a standard feature of the motif of dying and rising with Christ. The connection is shown not only by the contrast of life to crucifixion, but also by that of Spirit to flesh, the contrast which dominates the whole preceding section. The phrase ζῶμεν πνεύματι corresponds to similar constructions with the dative found in the other passages from the Pauline homologoumena discussed in Part I. We have interpreted this dative by speaking of living "to" a lord, in the sense of being under the dominion of or in service to that lord[3]. To be sure, the datives in Gal. 5 25 are related to the datives in 5 16 and 18, and this construction is connected in this passage with the thought of the Spirit as an active power which brings forth fruit. Therefore, while Gal. 5 25 uses a familiar construction, it is likely that the dative has more of an instrumental sense here than in other passages. However, this variation simply indicates another aspect of the same thing, for the lord under whom one stands not only demands obedience but also is at work in those under his dominion, who act through his power.

6. Galatians 6 14-15

In contrast to his opponents, who wish to boast "in your flesh," i. e., in the Galatians' circumcision, Paul declares that for him all boasting has been excluded, except in the cross of Christ. In the context this exclusion of boasting refers primarily to giving up reliance on the prerogatives of the Jew, including circumcision. However, the concept of "boasting" is an important one for Paul and has a wider significance. It refers to man's attitude of sinful self-reliance before God[1], and so is characteristic of life in the old dominion. The

---

[3] Cf. p. 18.
[1] Cf. BULTMANN, Theologie, pp. 242—43 (English: vol. 1, pp. 242—43). This concept is one expression of a basic aspect of Paul's understanding of sin. Cf. BULTMANN, pp. 237—246.

significance of this concept for Paul is especially clear in Rom. 3 27 and I Cor. 1 29. In Romans it is applied to the Jew, who "boasts in God," i. e., in his special relation to God, or "in the law" (2 17, 23). Then in 3 27, immediately after his initial explanation of what God has done in the death of Jesus, Paul brings out the significance of this event in this way: "Where, then, is the boasting (that I was previously talking about)?[2] It has been excluded." This is one of the most important consequences of God's act of justification "freely, by his grace" (3 24), and Paul immediately connects this to his emphasis on justification through faith. "It has been excluded. Through what kind of law? That of works? No, but through the law of faith." The way of works gives free rein to man's boast (4 2). Faith, when contrasted with works, is the opposite of this boastful self-reliance. It is the surrender of one's boast in the face of God's act of grace, which leaves no room for a boast before God. In Rom. 5 Paul again picks up the theme of boasting by speaking of the positive boast "in God" which takes the place of the boast of the old life (5 2-3, 11). In I Cor. 1 Paul also uses the concept of boasting to help explain what has taken place through the cross. There Paul speaks of both Jews and Greeks. For them the cross is an offense, for they judge it according to the wisdom and power of the world. In this cross, and in the subsequent call of the lowly, God has "made foolish the wisdom of the world" (vs. 20). This took place "in order that no flesh might boast before God" (vs. 29, cf. vs. 31). In God's "foolishness," his act of grace through the cross, the sin of the world, which is summed up in its boasting, is put to shame and destroyed. Thus the foundation of the old world is undercut, and the basis of a new life is laid.

In Gal. 6 14 the exclusion of boasting is connected with the crucifixion of the old world, for such boasting is an important characteristic of this old world. Paul now finds himself in a new world, and the only boasting which fits this new situation is boasting in the cross. This does not mean boasting anew in what one has attained. It means boasting only in God's act of grace. Crucifixion to the old world of boasting means a lasting separation from that world[3]. The only boasting which is left for the Christian is a boasting "in the Lord" (I Cor. 1 31) and a boasting "in weaknesses" (II Cor. 12 9), the very opposite of what was formerly the case.

Δι' οὗ in vs. 14 ("through which" or "through whom") probably refers to the cross, since Paul is speaking of the means of crucifixion. Even if this phrase should refer to Christ, it is apparent here

---

[2] Anaphoric article.
[3] Note the perfect ἐσταύρωται.

that it is Christ on the cross through whom Paul was crucified. Thus, it is particularly clear in Gal. 6 14 that it is directly in the cross of Christ that the believers' crucifixion took place. Just as in Rom. 7 4 and Gal. 2 19, an indirect participation in Christ's cross, mediated through a repetition or representation of that event, is excluded. And so this passage also supports the thesis that Christ's crucifixion is understood as an inclusive event.

Paul declares here that he was crucified to the world rather than to sin or the law. This is no fundamental difference, for Paul often uses the term κόσμος to refer to the present evil world, the world in which sin, death, and the law are the ruling powers. We have previously noted the eschatological connotation of the idea of the two dominions found in the passages we are discussing. This passage brings this cosmic-eschatological aspect to the forefront. This aspect must not be weakened by the interpreter, as, for instance, Ernest De Witt Burton does when he says that κόσμος in Gal. 6 14 means "the mode of life characterized by earthly advantages," and then explains that "Paul's world, κόσμος, with which he severed his relation ... was that of Israelitish descent, circumcision," etc.[4] The examples given by Burton do not substantiate his claim that κόσμος can simply mean a "mode of life." There is no instance in Paul's letters in which this word is used in the manner in which we speak of the Jewish "world" or the "world" of business. It cannot refer here, then, to one "mode of life" in the world which the individual may choose in contrast to other possible modes of life. Living to the world does, indeed, involve a particular "mode of life," but this mode of life is not one of several worldly possibilities open to the individual. Rather, the world has a structure which determines the life of each individual, and so human life as a whole, and man can only escape from this through an event which breaks into the all-encompassing world of sin and opens the possibility of a new existence in a new world. It is to such an eschatological event that Paul is referring when he speaks of the crucifixion of the world. The fact that Paul says that "the world has been crucified to *me*" cannot be taken as an indication that this is a matter of the individual's attitude or of subjective experience. Paul uses emphatic pronouns of the first person here because he is contrasting himself with his opponents[5]. There are some who do not at present share in this crucifixion to the world and consequent exclusion of boasting. This is not because it is merely

---

[4] A Critical and Exegetical Commentary on the Epistle to the Galatians, New York 1920, p. 354. Cf. p. 514.

[5] See especially the ἐμοί at the beginning of the verse. The familiar construction with dative should be noted. But unlike κόσμῳ here and the datives in other passages, ἐμοί does not refer to a lord or dominion.

subjective, but because the old world still continues in spite of the presence of the "new creation."[6]

To the old aeon as "world" is contrasted the new aeon as "new creation." Καινὴ κτίσις refers here not to the act of creation[7], but to its result[8], i. e., to the new created world. This is supported by the use of this phrase to refer to the result of the creative activity in II Cor. 5 17, its only other occurrence in the New Testament, and by the mention of the "world" in Gal. 6 14, which must be the old reality corresponding to the new. The fact that καινὴ κτίσις is also contrasted with "circumcision" and "uncircumcision" does not argue for an active sense, for these words indicate here the state of being circumcised or uncircumcised. Further, κτίσις here is probably to be translated "creation" rather than "creature." It is true that the latter is the better translation in II Cor. 5 17, though Paul there immediately slips into the broader meaning by speaking of τὰ ἀρχαῖα and καινά. But the reference to the destruction of the world in Gal. 6 14 is decisive for the translation "new creation" in vs. 15. The eschatological significance of this phrase is well established in the Pseudepigrapha[9]. At the consummation the old world passes away and the new creation comes. It is particularly clear in Gal. 6 14-15 that crucifixion with Christ involves an eschatological change from the old to the new aeon.

We find once again that against an insistence on the old, in this case circumcision, Paul makes use of the idea of dying with Christ to declare the eschatological newness of Christian existence. The distinctions, the values, and the boast of the old world no longer hold for the Christian, for he has been crucified to the old world and shares in the new creation.

7. *II Corinthians 5 14-17*

We now move on to a passage in which neither a construction with σύν nor the verb σταυρόω is applied to the Christian, but which, nevertheless, must be included in the group of passages which we

---

[6] Cf. pp. 75—79.

[7] So BURTON, Galatians, p. 356.

[8] So SCHLIER, Galater, *ad loc.*

[9] Cf. ethiopic Enoch 72 1, syriac Baruch 32 6, 44 12, 57 2; Jubilees 1 29, 4 26. Other references in TWNT, vol. 3, p. 1020, n. 144. The rabbis use the phrase "new creature" in a wider sense. Cf. HERMANN L. STRACK & PAUL BILLERBECK, Kommentar zum Neuen Testament aus Talmud und Midrasch, vol. 2, München 1924, pp. 421—22. But the accompanying idea of release from the κόσμος is decisive for the eschatological meaning in Gal. 6 14-15.

are discussing. In II Cor. 5 14 Paul makes an abrupt assertion followed by an inference which is equally abrupt: "One died for all. Therefore, all died." On what basis is Paul able to make this immediate inference from "one" to "all"? As Hans Windisch has pointed out, the idea of dying "for all" does not sufficiently explain this conclusion. Indeed, on this basis one would expect quite a different conclusion, such as: "Therefore, all were saved from death."[1] *Rescue* from death is clearly the implication when Paul speaks of those who "risked their neck for my life (ὑπὲρ τῆς ψυχῆς μου)" (Rom. 16 4). This is the significance of Jesus' death according to John 11 50: "It is advantageous for you that one man die for the people (ὑπὲρ τοῦ λαοῦ) and not the whole nation be destroyed." If the idea of a death "for all" does not sufficiently explain Paul's conclusion here, on what is it based? Windisch refers to dying with Christ, but leaves this idea undeveloped[2]. The following will supply evidence to support this assertion.

In vs. 15 the significance of vs. 14 is spelled out in terms which are familiar to us. Christ died "in order that those living might live no longer to themselves but to the one who died for them and was raised." Here we find the same construction of the verb ζάω with dative that we have found in other passages which refer to dying with Christ[3]. Paul speaks of living "to themselves" rather than to sin, but these are closely connected, as is shown by the important place which "boasting" occupies in Paul's understanding of sin[4]. Though this formulation does not in itself make clear that Paul is thinking about domination by the old aeon and its powers, as in previous passages, such ideas are suggested in the following verses, where he speaks of what has been left behind as "flesh" (vs. 16) and "the old world (τὰ ἀρχαῖα)" (vs. 17). With this old life Paul contrasts a new life "to the one who died for them and was raised." Thus in explaining the significance of the death of all which follows from the death of Christ, Paul speaks of a movement from one life to another, using the construction with ζάω and dative. This movement is precisely the concern of the other passages which we have examined, and is expressed by the same construction. In the other passages this movement takes place through dying with Christ. Here also reference to this transfer follows a statement which connects the death of Christ and the death of the believers: "One died for all. Therefore, all died." This is merely a different formulation of the motif of dying with Christ.

---

[1] Der Zweite Korintherbrief, 9. Aufl. Göttingen 1924, p. 182. See the references to passages and literature there.   [2] *Ibid.*, p. 181.
[3] Rom. 6 10-11, Gal. 2 19, 5 25. Cf. also Rom. 6 2, 7 4, Gal. 6 14.
[4] Cf. pp. 62—63.

In vs. 16 Paul draws a conclusion from his statement in vss. 14-15: "Therefore, from now on we know no one according to flesh." This assertion is based upon the transfer from the old life to the new which has taken place in that "all died." Now the old reality which has been left behind is described as "flesh," as in Rom. 7 5 and Gal. 5 24. "From now on" refers back to the decisive event through which the believer has entered the new life, i. e., to the fact that "one died for all; therefore, all died." Thus it does not refer primarily to the time of the individual's conversion, but rather to the time of God's decisive act which changed the situation of men in the world. Paul's use of the term "now" elsewhere supports this, for it frequently refers to the present age of the manifestation of God's righteousness, the time of salvation, in contrast to the time before God's decisive act[5]. Vs. 16 emphasizes strongly the difference of this "now" from the old manner of existence, and does so in a manner determined by the problem with which Paul is dealing. This verse has been described as a "Zwischensatz," interrupting the continuity of thought[6]. However, BULTMANN has shown that this verse draws from vss. 14-15 the particular consequence which is important for Paul at this point[7]. Since 2 14 Paul has been engaged in a defense of his apostleship. He is struggling to make clear his "sufficiency" (2 16, 3 5), the nature of his "confidence" (3 4), why he may act with "boldness" (3 12), need not despair (4 1, 16), and can be of good courage (5 6, 8). In all this Paul is struggling with the question of how, if at all, an apostle can commend himself before others (3 1ff., 5 12, 6 4). This is not an easy question, for Paul's sufficiency is not from himself, but from God (3 5). He cannot defend himself by pointing to human abilities and accomplishments. However, Paul can make one defense which the believers, at least, should be able to understand and accept. Paul points in chapter 3 to the exceeding measure of glory present in the new ministry of the Spirit. He points in chapter 4 to the "extraordinary power of God" which is manifest in the midst of constant participation in death. He points in 5 18ff. to the present action of God in carrying out his reconciling work through his ambassadors. Paul bases his "sufficiency," then, on the fact that the new aeon has broken in with its glory, and that the power of the salvation event is now at work in his proclamation and apostolic activity. Within this argument 5 14-17 also has its place. In 5 12 the

---

[5] Rom. 3 21, 26; 5 9, 11; 8 1; II Cor. 6 2.
[6] HANS LIETZMANN, An die Korinther I, II, 4. von W. G. Kümmel ergänzte Aufl. Tübingen 1949, p. 125.
[7] RUDOLF BULTMANN, Exegetische Probleme des Zweiten Korintherbriefes, Uppsala 1947, pp. 12—20. This holds at least for vs. 16a. The difficult problem of vs. 16b will not be dealt with here.

question of recommending oneself is again raised and Paul distinguishes himself from those who "boast in appearance." No outward, human standard of judgment is adequate. In vs. 13 he even rejects ecstatic phenomena as a relevant criterion. Any such judgment of his "sufficiency" fails to take into account the fact that "all died," that we live no longer to ourselves but to Christ. It fails to take into account the radical newness of Christian existence and the resulting exclusion of all human standards of judgment. The consequence is clear: we can no longer know anyone "according to flesh." This judgment according to flesh is the judgment which Paul's opponents have applied to him and in which he was found wanting. But these standards no longer hold. The argument is quite similar to that in Gal. 6 14-15. There boasting in the values of the old world is excluded because of crucifixion to the old world and participation in a new world. Here all judgment of Paul according to such values is excluded on the same basis.

Vs. 17 strengthens the connection which we have noted between this passage and Gal. 6 14-15, for here we have the only other occurrence in the New Testament of the phrase καινὴ κτίσις[8]. Vs. 17 deals with the same "before" and "after" as vss. 15-16, but now the preceding is broadened to a statement of the widest implications. Not only has the old knowing passed away, but with it the entire old world. Here the movement from the old to the new dominion, which we have found to be a constant feature of the passages examined in Part I, again appears in a form which brings the cosmic-eschatological aspect to the forefront, just as in Gal. 6 14-15. The singular τις suggests that καινὴ κτίσις is to be translated in the individual sense as "new creature." But for Paul there is only a new creature if there is a new world of which he is a part[9]. So vs. 17 quickly slips from the individual to the general. Τὰ ἀρχαῖα refers to the whole old world, which has become new[10]. This eschatological change must not be transformed into a subjective one, as if it were merely the individual's viewpoint which had changed. It is true that the new creation is manifest only to the one who is "in Christ." It is also true that for the time being the old world continues to exist alongside the new. But this is so even for the Christian, as we shall see. Thus this is not a matter of the individual's viewpoint, but of

---

[8] On the eschatological sense of this phrase see p. 65.
[9] Cf. my remarks on σῶμα, pp. 71—72.
[10] It is analogous to the phrase τὰ πάντα, which often means "the whole world, the universe." Cf. Rom. 11 36; I Cor. 8 6, 15 28; Gal. 3 22; Phil. 3 21. Furthermore, compare II Cor. 5 17 with Rev. 21 4-5. These two passages probably reflect a common apocalyptic tradition based on such passages as Isa. 43 18-19 and 65 17. The cosmic scope of the change is clear in Rev. 21.

the eschatological situation. If Paul were only able to assert that "for me" or "in my view" the old world has passed away, he would not be able to argue as he does that others may no longer judge him according to flesh, for they would be as entitled to their viewpoint as he to his. Paul's whole argument in these verses depends upon the reality of the presence of the new aeon.

W. G. KÜMMEL[11] and HEINZ-DIETRICH WENDLAND[12] refer to the idea of Christ as second Adam in connection with vs. 17. There may be some justification for this, for we occasionally find the phrase "in Christ" in connection with references to Christ as an inclusive person[13], and there is also evidence for a connection between the idea of new creation and that of an inclusive man[14]. The relation between "one" and "all" which is brought out in vs. 14 may also be compared to the relation between "one" and "all" or "one" and "many" which is so important in Rom. 5 12ff. If this idea is in the background of Paul's thought here, it is simply another instance of the connection which we have already noted between the motif of dying with Christ and such inclusive patterns of thought.

We have found that vs. 14 has the same significance as Paul's references to dying with Christ elsewhere. It is accompanied by the same idea of a decisive change from an old life to a new life under a new lord, and this is expressed by the same construction. We have found that II Cor. 5 14-17 is especially close to Gal. 6 14-15, both in terms of its argument against judgment according to the values of the old world and in its emphasis on the cosmic-eschatological nature of the change which has taken place. We must conclude, then, that the basis for the direct inference from the death of one to the death of all in vs. 14 is the idea of dying with Christ.

One of the unusual aspects of this passage is the close connection of dying with Christ to Christ's death "for all" in vss. 14-15. Although the idea of Christ's death "for all" as used in the New Testament does not sufficiently explain the inference in vs. 14, Christ's death for all and the death of all in that death have become very closely connected in Paul's mind[15].

---

[11] In LIETZMANN, Korinther, p. 205.
[12] Die Briefe an die Korinther, 8. Aufl. Göttingen 1962, p. 181.
[13] Cf. I Cor. 15 22, Gal. 3 26-28.
[14] Cf. Eph. 2 15, 4 24; Col. 3 10. This reflects a baptismal tradition with which Paul shows his acquaintance at Rom. 6 6. Cf. pp. 52—54.
[15] We will find a similar connection in I Thes. 5 10. See pp. 133—34.

8. Conclusion

The passages discussed above make clear that Paul's use of dying and rising with Christ must be understood in the context of his eschatology. This motif is used to indicate the decisive transfer of the believers from the old to the new aeon which has taken place in the death of Christ as an inclusive event. ALBERT SCHWEITZER also emphasized the importance of eschatology for understanding what he called Paul's "Mystik," within which he included dying and rising with Christ[1]. SCHWEITZER's treatment of the problem we are studying has already been criticized in a general way[2], and those who are familiar with his work will recognize that we have approached the problem in quite a different way and have come to different results on important points. However, SCHWEITZER's emphasis on the eschatological background of Paul's thought enabled him to show that Paul's "Mystik" transcends the individual and subjective[3]. This was an important contribution. Through what we have discovered in Part I SCHWEITZER's insight on this point is put on a more solid basis. The significance of this will become clearer as we note that the understanding of dying and rising with Christ developed above excludes certain dangerous misunderstandings.

Dying with Christ is misunderstood when it is thought to mean only that the believer repeats what Christ did. *As* Christ died to the old world *so* the believer dies to the old world, either by his own decision or in baptism[4]. In this interpretation the crucial significance for Paul of the death and resurrection of *Christ* is badly obscured. Christ becomes only a type of what happens to others more or less independently. The connection of dying and rising with Christ to Paul's eschatology makes clear that there is no possibility for the individual to die and rise in such independence of the Christ event. The individual is under the dominion of the powers of the old age. He is unable to free himself by himself. Only God's eschatological act, an act by which the old world is invaded and a new life in a new world is created, can free man from this slavery. Such an act involves the old world and new world as wholes. It takes place only once — in the death and resurrection of Christ, and it is to the believer's participation in these eschatological events that dying and rising with Christ refers. Even the idea that baptism supplements

---

[1] Die Mystik des Apostels Paulus.   [2] Cf. p. 5..
[3] Cf. Mystik, pp. 100—101 (English: 99—100).
[4] Such is the interpretation of THEODOR ZAHN, who paraphrases Rom. 6 5 in this way: "Wir sind mit dem Tode Christi als dem Typus eines damit vergleichbaren eigenen Erlebnisses so enge verbunden geworden, als ob wir mit ihm zusammengewachsen wären." Der Brief des Paulus an die Römer, Leipzig 1910, p. 300.

8. Conclusion

the death and resurrection of Christ by making it possible for the believer to participate in them obscures the significance of these events for Paul. In referring to the believers' past death with Christ, Paul is speaking directly of the significance of the cross. The participation of the believers in this event is not founded upon a unique power in the baptismal rite. It is founded upon the fact that the cross is itself an eschatological and inclusive event.

Dying and rising with Christ is also misunderstood when dissolved into a subjective, mystical experience. For a long time ADOLF DEISSMANN's emphasis on "Christ-mysticism" was influential in the interpretation of Paul. The religion of Paul was at its heart "Mystik" and "Mystik" was defined in this way: "I . . . give the name *Mystik* to every religious tendency that discovers the way to God direct through inner experience without the mediation of reasoning."[5] Dying and rising with Christ was interpreted accordingly, being understood as Paul's "passion-mysticism." This was meant to refer, first of all, to the way in which Paul understood his own sufferings, but DEISSMANN also included "the mystical meaning" of baptism. In connection with these ideas DEISSMANN felt that "the intimacy of this mystical contemplation of the passion" was plain[6]. We have yet to discuss the use of dying and rising with Christ in connection with Paul's suffering. In Part II it will be argued that this use of the motif must also be understood in the light of Paul's eschatology. However, it is plain that this emphasis on the subjective experience of the individual is far from the meaning of the texts discussed so far. Paul does not isolate the individual and focus upon his inner experience. He understands the individual as part of a world which determines his existence. Everything depends on the reality of release from the powers of the old world and incorporation in a new world. Only if there is a new world is the individual in a position to exist in a new way. Paul asserts that a new world has been created with the death and resurrection of Christ, and dying with Christ expresses the believer's inclusion in this movement from the old world to the new.

The importance of these ideas is underlined by the fact that a significant aspect of Paul's anthropology corresponds to this eschatology. This comes out in Paul's use of the term σῶμα ("body"). For Paul this term refers to man in his openness to that which is outside himself. Man as body is man-in-relation. He is open to be essentially conditioned by his participation in what is larger than himself. Σῶμα is not that which distinguishes one person from another, but that which relates him to others and which forms the basis of a

---

[5] *Paul*, p. 149.   [6] *Ibid.*, pp. 181—83.

self-determining participation in self-transcending realities[6a]. Thus σῶμα is clearly man in his physicalness, i. e., in his connection to the outside world and interaction with it. Σῶμα is especially used to refer to the self in sexual relations (Rom. 1 24, cf. 4 19). What a sexual relation means to Paul comes out most clearly in I Cor. 6 12ff., where it is described as a clinging or a joining so that two become one. Σῶμα is, then, this self which joins to what is outside itself and becomes part of a larger unity. The same idea comes out in I Cor. 7 4, with the important additional thought that this joining involves placing the σῶμα under the authority of someone or something. This is related to the use of σῶμα as the object of the rule of some power, such as sin. Σῶμα is what the power rules in, what it uses as its weapons, what it owns (Rom. 6 12, I Cor. 6 19). Σῶμα exists *for* or *to* something or someone (I Cor. 6 13). It is determined by what has power over it. It is a body of death (Rom. 7 24) or a body of sin (Rom. 6 6). That this involves domination by a power is shown by the fact that destruction of the body of sin results in release from slavery to sin (Rom. 6 6). The σώματα are members of a larger unity (I Cor. 6 15). Moreover, σῶμα can be the unity itself. Thus the prostitute and the one who joins himself to her become one σῶμα (I Cor. 6 16). This ties in naturally with the corporate sense of σῶμα, as in Paul's references to the body of Christ, but this involves special problems which cannot be treated here. The evidence above indicates that Paul sees man in his openness to the world outside him. Man is determined by the world within which he stands. The individual becomes what he is through that which has power over him. This does not mean that man has no freedom to determine his own existence, for, since God's act in Christ, man is faced with the choice of standing within one of two dominions. However, this choice is possible only because of God's eschatological act. Furthermore, it is the world-determining powers which pose this choice, and man does not have the choice of standing aloof. Thus for Paul the individual's fate is tied up with what God does with the *world*, and so his salvation is tied up with eschatology[7].

[6a] Cp. EDUARD SCHWEIZER, TWNT, vol. 7, pp. 1062—63.

[7] ERNST KÄSEMANN has seen this relation between Paul's anthropology and his eschatology clearly and has emphasized the importance of this for understanding Paul. Cf. Exegetische Versuche, vol. 1, p. 19: "Menschliche Existenz ruht für ihn [Paul] nicht mehr in ihr selbst, sie ist durch die Verflochtenheit mit ihrer Welt bestimmt, Objekt des Kampfes himmlischer und irdischer Mächte und Schauplatz dieses Kampfes. Existenz wird dadurch qualifiziert, welcher Macht man gehört, welchen Herrn man hat." When this is clear, it is also clear that "die paulinische Anthropologie ist ... die Tiefendimension der paulinischen Kosmologie und Eschatologie." RGG, vol. 2, col. 1275.

8. Conclusion

In the Introduction it was pointed out that RUDOLF BULTMANN gives an important place to the motif of dying and rising with Christ in his explanation of Paul's view of Christ's death and resurrection as salvation event. He does so because he feels that one must answer the question of how the salvation event can be understood as directed at man, reaching him, and happening to him[8]. By the patterns of thought which we have been investigating Paul makes clear that the salvation event does actually happen to men[9]. Thus to respond to the proclamation by acknowledging the crucified one as Lord means, at the same time, to let oneself be crucified with Christ[10]. BULTMANN is correct in giving an important place to dying and rising with Christ at this point, for we have seen that Paul uses this motif to say something fundamental about the saving significance of Christ's death and resurrection. However, BULTMANN has been accused of jeopardizing the uniqueness and finality of the saving events. Symptomatic of what his critics fear are BULTMANN's assertions that "das Heilsgeschehen nirgends anders als im verkündigenden, im anredenden, fordernden und verheißenden Wort präsent ist"[11] and that "Tod Christi ein 'kosmisches' Ereignis ist, d. h. ... von ihm nicht mehr nur als von dem historischen Ereignis der Kreuzigung Jesu auf Golgatha geredet werden darf. Dieses Ereignis hat Gott ja zum eschatologischen Ereignis gemacht, so daß es, aller zeitlichen Begrenztheit entnommen, sich in jeder Gegenwart weiter vollzieht, im verkündigenden Wort wie in den Sakramenten."[12] BULTMANN's use of dying and rising with Christ seems to contribute to the danger to which his critics point. This danger must be avoided. It is avoided when dying and rising with Christ is understood in the manner indicated in Part I, for then it is clear that Paul is speaking of Christ's death on Golgotha as an event which concerns the old and new dominions, and so the many individuals who exist within them. Through his use of this motif Paul brings out *both* the uniqueness and finality of the past saving events *and* the direct involvement of the believer's existence in these events. Thus a proper understanding of this motif opens up the possibility of preserving some of the values of BULTMANN's approach while clearly avoiding the danger of which his opponents are afraid.

Recognition of the full implications of what we have been learning will require important modifications in BULTMANN's interpretation of Paul. BULTMANN's treatment of σῶμα is symptomatic of a

---

[8] Theologie, pp. 302, 294. (Page numbers of vol. 1 of the English edition correspond closely to the German.)
[9] *Ibid.*, p. 300.
[10] *Ibid.*, p. 303.
[11] *Ibid.*, p. 301.   [12] *Ibid.*, p. 303.

significant weakness in his interpretation of Paul. BULTMANN emphasizes that the term σῶμα shows that man, according to Paul, is "ein Wesen, das ein Verhältnis zu sich selbst hat, das sich selbst überantwortet und für sein Sein verantwortlich ist."[13] As comparison with the interpretation of σῶμα above will show, this is much too individualistic. Furthermore, this mistake is accompanied by a failure to see the importance of the cosmic or suprapersonal aspects of Paul's eschatology[14]. If Paul sees man as conditioned by the world of which he is a part, as argued above, man's salvation is tied up with what God does with this world. Thus history cannot be reduced to the historicity of the individual, and the cosmic aspects of Paul's eschatology cannot be dismissed as cosmological speculation. Finally, this makes clear that the future aspects of Paul's eschatology are essential also, another point at which BULTMANN's interpretation is weak[15]. The new world and its salvation are already present, but they are hidden in the midst of the old world. The believer cannot be isolated from this old world. He continues to suffer under its attacks, particularly through his body, which has not yet been transformed. The believers groan while awaiting the redemption of the body, which is tied up with the redemption of the whole creation (Rom. 8 18-23). Christian existence is existence in hope, and this hope is not merely "das Frei- und Offensein für die Zukunft,"[16] a quality which would be valid in itself. Rather, it is dependent on a future act of God, which will bring his saving work to its completion.

The passages which we have investigated in Part I emphasize the *newness* of the Christian situation. The powers of the old world no longer enslave the Christian (Rom. 6 2ff., 7 1ff., Gal. 2 19, 5 24), and he is no longer bound by the values and judgments of the old world (Gal. 6 14, II Cor. 5 14ff.). He now walks in newness of life (Rom. 6 4), or of Spirit (Rom. 7 6). Christ now lives in him (Gal. 2 20). He lives by the Spirit (Gal. 5 25). He is a new creature (Gal. 6 15, II Cor. 5 17). However, in the passages to be considered in Part II we will find Paul emphasizing his *continuing* participation in the death of Jesus, a participation which makes clear that the fullness of salvation is *not yet*. This emphasis is not meant to contradict what Paul says in the passages we have already discussed, but it does add an important qualification. It makes clear that the present participation in new life continues to be a participation in life through death, so that the believer must still rely upon God to grant this life in daily existence and at the resurrection.

---

[13] *Ibid.*, pp. 226—27. Cf. pp. 193—203.
[14] Cf. The Presence of Eternity: History and Eschatology, New York 1957, pp. 42—43.
[15] *Ibid.* [16] Theologie, p. 320.

Part II

Dying and Rising with Christ as the Structure of the New Life

In Part II we will consider those passages in which Paul refers to dying with Christ as a present aspect of Christian action and suffering. In these passages rising with Christ is both a present participation in the life of Christ and a future hope. That Paul uses the motif of dying and rising with Christ to interpret present Christian existence as well as to refer to a past event is an interesting fact. This indicates that the present structure of the new dominion corresponds to the events on which it is founded, for the death and resurrection of Christ continue to determine the life of the believer.

It is not immediately apparent why Paul should use the motif of dying and rising with Christ to speak of present Christian existence as well as of a decisive event of the past. The passages which speak of a present dying with Christ in suffering form a class quite distinct from the passages already discussed[1]. To be sure, the passages which refer to a past dying with Christ are not merely concerned with the past. The past death with Christ is important because it is the foundation of a new existence. The present existence of the Christian can only be understood by referring to this decisive, past event. Thus Paul relates the past and present of the Christian life very closely. However, to speak of a present *dying* with Christ after asserting that the believer *has* died with Christ might appear to be contradictory. If the believer has already died with Christ in a decisive event, how can he continue to do so in the present? If he has already been released from the old dominion through death, what importance can a present dying with Christ have? Such questions fail to take account of Paul's complex eschatology. The connection of dying and rising with Christ to Paul's eschatology was found to be important in Part I. This connection will also help us to understand the significance of the passages we will consider in Part II. Paul's eschatology is the result of a transformation of traditional ideas in the light of the new situation of the Christian. Paul had to come to grips with two facts: 1) The decisive event has already taken place, an event which Paul understood in eschatological terms. 2) Nevertheless, the old world continues to exist and to exercise a certain power. Both

---

[1] We do find ideas closely related to those in the passages discussed above in Phil. 3 3-11. Cf. pp. 115—16.

of these facts are related to essential interests of Paul. If the significance of the former were lost, Christ's death and resurrection would lose their importance, there would no longer be anything essentially new about the Christian's situation, and Paul would not be able to assert against the Judaizers that the Christian has died with Christ to the law. If the significance of the latter were lost, Christianity would degenerate into the kind of spiritualism which Paul battled at Corinth, a spiritualism for which salvation is already present in such a way that one can boast in it (I Cor. 4 5-8), for which the future resurrection and Christ's reign over the world are unimportant because the world and the body have no part in this salvation (cf. I Cor. 15), for which "all things are lawful" because the "belly" or body will perish and so its appetites are a matter of indifference to the spiritual man (I Cor. 6 12-13). The passages discussed in Part I emphasize that the decisive event has already taken place. The passages which we will consider in Part II carry with them the realization that the Christian is still exposed to the powers of the old aeon. This means that the two sets of passages stand in a certain tension with each other. This tension reflects the fundamental tension in Paul's eschatology. Neither aspect can be eliminated without seriously damaging Paul's understanding of Christian existence.

This tension cannot be resolved by asserting that Paul is simply talking about two different things. In the passages to be discussed in Part II we find, among other formulations, the same use of σύν as in Part I[2], and there are other formal similarities between the two sets of passages[3]. Furthermore, it is clear that there is an essential connection between these two uses of the one motif. When Paul speaks of Christian suffering as dying with Christ, he indicates that through this present participation in Christ's death the Christian is forced to give up all trust in himself and to trust in God alone. This theme will help us understand the relation of dying and rising with Christ to Paul's emphasis on justification through faith. Moreover, this trust in self is related to man's "boast"[4] and is characteristic of the existence of the old world. Thus the end of trust in self is an aspect of the break with the old world which is emphasized in the passages discussed in Part I. The fact that in both cases it is a question of this break with the old world makes clear the connection of the two groups of passages and requires us to understand them in relation to each other.

The passages to be discussed below, then, have something further to say about the eschatological fulfillment referred to in the

---

[2] Cf. II Cor. 4 14, 7 3, 13 4; Rom. 8 17.
[3] See the initial description of the motif on p. 6.
[4] Cf. Gal. 6 14 and pp. 62—63 above.

passages already discussed. They make clear that the new life in which the believer already participates continues to have the character of life-in-death. This means that the Christian still longs for the redemption which is to come. However, as long as the old world exists and the Christian is threatened by its powers, this continuing participation in death has a positive function in God's plan. Because they prevent the believer from trusting in himself and so falling back into the old life, suffering and death are positive aspects of God's rule over his own, and can be understood as participation in Christ's death. God has already conquered death, not by abolishing it (this is still future), but by commandeering it for his own purposes.

A. DYING AND RISING WITH CHRIST IN ETHICAL ACTION

Although the passages in which Paul speaks of dying and rising with Christ in connection with suffering are distinct from the passages which refer to dying with Christ as a past event, there is no such separation between past and present when Paul uses this motif in connection with his ethical exhortation. Passages which we have already discussed, especially Rom. 6 and Gal. 5 24-25, connect this motif with such exhortation. However, the previous discussion did not deal adequately with the significance of this motif for Paul's understanding of the ongoing life of the Christian. This section will carry further the discussion of Rom. 6, and supplement it by a discussion of Rom. 8 10-13. In so doing it will make clear that the theme of dying with Christ is not only used by Paul to refer to the past event on which the Christian's life is based but also shapes his exhortation, and that an understanding of dying and rising with Christ helps us to understand the theological foundations of Paul's exhortation.

It has frequently been noted that Paul can connect an imperative with an indicative of the same content. We find this in its most developed form in Rom. 6[1]. The whole chapter receives its structure from the linking of imperative with indicative. The exhortation which begins with vs. 11 is based upon the previous argument that the believers have died with Christ to sin, and reflects the same patterns of thought. In vss. 8-10 Paul asserts first that the believers have died with Christ, and then that Christ has died to sin once for all. Instead of continuing in the indicative by stating that "you also are dead to sin," in vs. 11 Paul exhorts: "Thus you also reckon yourselves to be dead to sin." This "reckoning" does not merely refer to how the

---

[1] Cf. also I Cor. 5 7, Gal. 5 25, and Rom. 8 9-13.

believers are to view themselves, but also to the active manifestation of this deadness to sin, as is shown by what follows. Similarly, in vs. 6 Paul asserts that through crucifixion with Christ the believers have been released from slavery to sin. In vs. 12 he exhorts: "Therefore, do not let sin reign in your mortal body." Thus Paul begins his exhortation by making use of the same patterns of thought as in his previous discussion of the believers' past death to the old dominion[2]. Furthermore, this exhortation is presented as a logical inference from the preceding discussion (vs. 11: οὕτως; vs. 12: οὖν). The indicative of death to sin somehow implies the imperative of death to sin. It is quite clear here (and in the other passages in which indicative and imperative are directly linked) that this is not due to an unconscious slip on Paul's part. The linking of the two elements is deliberate. We will see more clearly what is behind this striking pattern of thought as we investigate the significance of the motif of dying and rising with Christ for Paul's exhortation.

It might seem that, if the indicative were really meant, the imperative would not be necessary. However, the fact that the indicative still implies an imperative is rooted deeply in Paul's thought, being related to the fundamental tension in Paul's eschatology[3]. As we saw when considering the term σῶμα, Paul sees man together with his world[4]. There can be no redemption of man, or a part of man, apart from the transformation of the world which conditions his existence. The new world is already present, but it is hidden within the old. The full influence of the new Lord upon concrete, physical life is not yet manifest. The redemption of the body is tied up with the redemption of the physical creation, and this is still an object of hope and longing (Rom. 8 19-23). The corruption which enslaves creation as a whole also enslaves the body, and so the believers still eagerly await "the redemption of our body"[5] (8 20-23). The body is not only still subject to death. It continues to be a point of battle between sin and God, for both claim it and demand its obedience. According to Rom. 6 12, not only is the body still mortal, but its "desires" are still on the side of sin's reign. However, the Lord also lays claim to the body. This is not a matter of indifference, as if the believer could be saved apart from his physical life. It is through the body that the believer acts. To whom the believer presents himself as a slave through acts of obedience determines whose slave he is (6 16), and so it is possible for a believer to again become a slave of

---

[2] See also vss. 16-19, where the exhortation to "present your members in servitude" is connected with the fact that the believers have been enslaved.

[3] Cf. above, pp. 75—77.

[4] Cf. pp. 71—72.

[5] This is not to be translated "redemption *from* our body." Cp. Rom. 8 11.

sin through acts of sinning. It is against this possibility that Paul must direct his exhortation: "Present ... your members to God as weapons of righteousness" (6 13).

In Rom. 8 10-13 the body is spoken of in a way which is similar to Rom. 6 12. It is clear that the body is still under the power of death, for it is described as "dead" (vs. 10) or "mortal" (vs. 11). This is "because of sin" (vs. 10). In the continuing subjection of the body to death, sin continues to make its power felt[6]. In vs. 13 the body is seen as standing entirely on the side of flesh, for the deeds of the body must be put to death[7]. In contrast to the deadness of the body, the new reality of "life" is already present (vs. 10). However, this does not mean that man's redemption is fully accomplished, that he has been saved apart from his body. Rather, the fact that the body has not yet been redeemed means that man has not yet been fully redeemed. So Paul adds in vs. 11 that the presence of the Spirit is also the guarantee of the resurrection of the body. God will redeem the body also, although at present the body still feels the power of the old world.

Just as in Rom. 6, recognition of the fact that the body is still exposed to the power of sin is accompanied by exhortation. The exhortation in vss. 12-13 is based upon the preceding argument that the believers are no longer in flesh but in Spirit. Again it is a matter of drawing the imperative from the indicative: because they are no longer in flesh, they must no longer live according to the flesh. The idea of being "debtors" is related to the imagery of slavery and legal bondage in Rom. 6 and 7 1-6, and the contrast of the two results of death and life in vs. 13 is related to the similar thought in 6 21-23. The connection with Rom. 6 is especially clear from the fact that the "deeds of the body" are spoken of as being "put to death (θανατοῦτε)." Here we see the influence of the idea of dying with Christ. This is indicated by the similarities between this verse and Rom. 6 11-12 and Gal. 5 24-25. It is also shown by the context. Vs. 13 contrasts death and life. Paul is conscious of a connection between the life of which he is speaking and the resurrection of Jesus, for vs. 11, in speaking of the resurrection of the believers' bodies, relates this to Jesus' resurrection by referring to God as the source of both. Furthermore, vss. 14-17 connect vs. 13 with the motif of dying and rising with Christ expressed in a familiar pattern. Vss. 14-17 support

---

[6] Subjection to the power of sin and the power of death are very closely connected in Paul's mind. Cf. Rom. 5 12, 21; I Cor. 15 56.

[7] However, it is doubtful that σῶμα is simply equivalent to the evil power "flesh" in this verse. This is certainly not the case in vss. 10-11. It could not be said that flesh is dead "because of sin." This would be reason for it to be alive. Further, note the reference to the resurrection of the body.

the assertion "you will live" in vs. 13[8]. The conclusion which Paul wishes to make through his argument is clear in vs. 17. Through the Spirit the believers are children of God and so heirs, that is, heirs of the glory of the resurrection life, as the following makes clear, and so the assertion in vs. 13 has been supported. But for Paul this means being "Christ's fellow heirs, if, indeed, we are suffering with him in order that we might also be glorified with him." Here the motif of dying and rising with Christ is clearly expressed[9]. Paul draws the conclusion which supports vs. 13 in terms of dying and rising with Christ, and thereby indicates that this thought was already present in vs. 13. The presence of this motif explains the fact that Paul speaks of "putting to death" the deeds of the body, a formulation which would be rather strange if we were not already familiar with this motif.

After recognizing that Rom. 8 13 reflects the idea of dying and rising with Christ, we need also to recognize that there are some significant differences between the way in which the motif is used here and the way in which it was used in the passages discussed in Part I. Instead of being a past event, the dying referred to is a continuing process in the believer's life. Moreover, this takes place "by the Spirit." Here the Spirit has an active killing function. Through the Spirit what took place decisively in the death of Christ continually takes place: the believer dies to the old life "according to flesh." We have seen above why this must be so. The believer is still a part of an untransformed world and through the body is subject to the attacks of the old powers. In the face of such attacks, the believer's past death with Christ must be maintained and affirmed in the present. Thus the believer's existence continues to be characterized by dying with Christ.

Because of this, existence in the new dominion takes on a structure which corresponds to the founding events of death and resurrection, and there is a sense in which we can say that the Christian *continually* dies with Christ. However, what we learned in Part I makes clear that this cannot mean that Christ dies over and over, nor that the believer has a number of "experiences" of the death of Jesus which are all roughly on the same level. Rather, Christ died "once for all" (Rom. 6 10) and the believers were included in that event. The priority and uniqueness of Christ's death on the cross is clear. The present dying of the believer does not repeat that event but is based upon it. The new dominion is founded only once, even though the whole of the new dominion participates in the founding

---

[8] So also Kuss, Römerbrief, p. 599.
[9] On Rom. 8 17 see pp. 112—14.

A. Dying and Rising with Christ in Ethical Action

events and the existence of the individual continues to be shaped by these events. In order to make clear that the present dying of the believer is always based upon these past events, we should say that the believer continually dies with Christ in that there takes place in his life a continual manifestation and affirmation of his past death with Christ.

Understanding the theological foundations of Paul's exhortation is a central problem in the interpretation of Pauline theology. If Paul's exhortation is cut off from his soteriology, it is hard to avoid the conclusion that Paul either reinstated the way of works in order to have an ethical norm, thereby destroying his own theology, or attributed no decisive significance to the Christian's actions, thereby destroying the foundation of his exhortation. However, Paul lays the foundation for his exhortation very carefully in Rom. 6 and 8 1-13, and in Rom. 12 1-2 he begins his exhortation by reminding the reader of this foundation[10]. Rom. 6 makes clear that Paul understands his exhortation to be directly related to basic soteriological conceptions. This is emphasized by the way in which Paul bases his imperative upon a similar indicative. This indicates that Paul's exhortation is not a fragment, but is founded upon his understanding of the saving events.

What we have learned about the motif of dying and rising with Christ helps us to understand how Paul can base imperative on indicative. By means of this motif Paul makes clear that the ongoing life of the believer is directly related to what took place in the saving events. As we have seen, dying with Christ means dying to the old dominion of sin and entry into a new dominion. The actions of the individual reflect his participation in the dominion of which he is a part, for each of the two dominions has certain "works" or "fruit" which are characteristic of it (cf. Gal. 5 19-23). Thus the transfer from the old dominion to the new which takes place through dying with Christ will manifest itself in the actions of the believer. In this way Paul makes clear that the eschatological change which has taken place in Christ's death will have its effect in daily life. To be sure, there is a continuing struggle against the powers of the old dominion. Furthermore, the believer is not simply dragged along by the Spirit as if he had no choice. The believer is actively enlisted in the struggle. He is *exhorted* to not let sin reign in his body, and this exhortation is a serious matter, for by sinning the believer can fall back into the old slavery to sin (cf. Rom. 6 16). However, the believer's situation is quite different than it was before dying with Christ. He has not

---

[10] Rom. 12 1: "Present your bodies" — cp. 6 12-13, 19. Rom. 12 2: "Do not be conformed to this age" — cp. the idea of the two dominions in Rom. 6 and 8 1-13.

only been released from his former slavery. He has been enslaved to a new master. He does not exist in a vacuum any more than he did before. The believer is not left without protection against the powers of the old dominion, for a new power determines his life, a power by which he is able to "put to death the deeds of the body" (Rom. 8 13). This enslavement of the believer to a new power must not be forgotten, for it is an essential part of Paul's conception. Nor should we underestimate this power. The believer can only escape from it if the death and resurrection of Christ cease to determine his life, so that it can no longer be said that he has died with Christ.

It is important to recognize that this enslavement to a new power is not an optional event which comes after the believer has been released from sin. One is not freed from sin and then, perhaps, also put under a new Lord. Rather, these are two aspects of the same event. As we have seen, Paul sees man as part of his world. He does not conceive of man as able to exist as an isolated individual, and so there can be no intermediate state between release from the old dominion and entry into the new. Man can be saved only if he is released from the powers of the old dominion, but he is released from these powers only if he is placed under a new Lord. Thus man is saved *because* he has a new Lord. What God gives to man through Christ *is* himself as Lord[11]. This makes clear that Paul's "ethics" cannot be separated from his understanding of salvation. Paul's exhortation simply concerns the concrete manifestation of the new lordship through which one is saved.

These considerations also help us to understand the meaning of the imperative which Paul bases on an indicative. This imperative does not indicate that man must now realize in fact what has been declared to be true in principle, for Paul makes no such distinction. Rather, this imperative means: allow God's lordship over you to manifest itself in your will and actions. And that also means: hold fast to the Lord who has been given to you; remain in his lordship. The seriousness of this imperative is clear, for, while the Christian's actions are not "works" which give him a claim on God's salvation, the Christian can fall away from the Lord through whom he is saved by allowing himself to be enslaved again by the old powers.

At the risk of oversimplifying Paul's complex thought, some indication must be given of another aspect of the theological basis of Paul's ethics, for there is danger that the references above to "dominions" and "powers" be dismissed as a speculative mythology for which there is no corresponding reality in the life of the individual.

---

[11] Cf. ERNST KÄSEMANN, "Gottesgerechtigkeit bei Paulus," ZThK 58 (1961), pp. 367—378.

This would not do justice to Paul's thought, for the fact that Christ's death is the basis for a new "walk" by the believer can also be explained in concrete terms. As we have seen, Paul can sum up man's sin by speaking of his "boast."[12] This sinful self-reliance is expressed in man's desire to be saved by his own achievements. This is a form of idolatry, for through this sinful boast men have refused to "glorify God as God or give thanks" to him (Rom. 1 21). They have "worshiped . . . the creature instead of the Creator" (Rom. 1 25). In Rom. 1 21-32 Paul connects man's idolatry with a life of vice. Because of their idolatry, God "hands over" men to a life of vice, and this means the disruption of man's relations with his fellow man. In Rom. 1 this is simply understood as God's judgment. However, we can see why this takes place, for the sinful boast which characterizes man's life expresses itself in his relations to other men as well as in his relation to God. Man exalts himself at the expense of others. Thus life according to flesh is characterized by the fact that men "bite and devour one another," the very opposite of love for the neighbor (Gal. 5 13-15), and Paul's exhortations to mutual love and helpfulness are interspersed with commands to not think too highly of oneself[13]. In I Cor. 4 6-7 Paul attributes the dissension in Corinth to such boasting, and he also points to the fact which should bring this boasting to an end, the fact that what the Corinthians have they have "received." Recognition by the Christian that his life is based on God's grace, not his own accomplishments, means the end of boasting. This makes clear how Christ's cross brings to an end the believer's old life and brings about a new life of a different kind. The cross, as God's act of grace, excludes man's boast (Rom. 3 27). The recognition of God's grace through faith means the surrender of man's boast. This results in a new kind of life, for the believer's previous "walk" was based upon his boast. In his relations to his fellow man, the end of this boast means the end of biting and devouring one another and the beginning of a new life characterized by serving one another through love (Gal. 5 13-15). Thus the believer's response to God's act of grace has direct consequences for ethical behavior, as Paul indicates when he speaks of "faith working through love" (Gal. 5 6). Therefore, the death of Christ is the foundation of a new manner of life for the believer and continues to exercise power over him and to determine his actions. Paul expresses this by speaking of the believer's death with Christ to sin as a decisive transfer to a new slavery and of a continuing participation in Christ's death through which "the deeds of the body" are "put to death."

---

[12] Cf. pp. 62—63. Paul can express the same understanding of sin in other ways. Cf. p. 124.

[13] Rom. 12 3, 16; Gal. 5 26, 6 3-4. Cf. I Cor. 8 1, 13 4-5.

B. DYING AND RISING WITH CHRIST IN SUFFERING

1. II Corinthians 4 7-14

In II Cor. 4 10 Paul refers to his participation in both the νέκρωσις τοῦ 'Ιησοῦ and the ζωὴ τοῦ 'Ιησοῦ. In speaking of the νέκρωσις τοῦ 'Ιησοῦ, Paul is referring to Jesus' own death or dying as something in which the apostle shares, and the ζωὴ τοῦ 'Ιησοῦ refers in a similar way to Jesus' resurrection life. This is supported by the fact that in Rom. 4 19, Mark 3 5 (D), and Hermas Sim. 9, 16, 2f. the genitive dependent on νέκρωσις in each case indicates that which is dead or dying. Furthermore, the other passages to be discussed in this section will make abundantly clear that Paul interprets his suffering in terms of participation in Christ's death and resurrection. This can be expressed by formulations with σύν similar to those which we have previously encountered[1]. The connection of II Cor. 4 10-12 with such formulations is shown by vs. 14. Thus it is clear that Paul is using the same motif here as in the passages already discussed.

The extraordinary power of which Paul is aware is shown to be God's power, not his own, in the concrete experiences of his life. In these experiences Paul is continually being pushed to the brink of total destruction. He stands helpless under an overwhelming pressure and his own power is exhausted. The fact that he is nevertheless preserved, that again and again a way is opened for him to step back from the brink, can only be understood by Paul as miracle, that is, a manifestation of the power of God quite apart from his own power. Vss. 8-9 develop this experience by a series of paired participles dependent on vs. 7, with the second of each pair indicating the extreme form of the first. From this extreme form Paul has been miraculously preserved through the power of God. Vs. 10 is also dependent on vs. 7, adding one more participle to the series in vss. 8-9. Like vss. 7-9 it relates Paul's suffering to the manifestation of divine power in the midst of that suffering. However, instead of merely contrasting his suffering and preservation, Paul in vs. 10 returns to the formulation of vs. 7, for the positive aspect is related to the suffering and weakness by means of a ἵνα clause. The "life of Jesus" of which Paul speaks in vs. 10 corresponds to the "power of God" of vs. 7. Just as the power of God manifests itself in the experiences of physical deliverance summed up in vss. 8-9, so this "life of Jesus" manifests itself "in our body," that is, in these same experiences of physical deliverance. Thus the "life of Jesus" is another way of referring to

---
[1] Cf. Rom. 8 17; II Cor. 7 3, 13 4.

this divine power. This is supported by the fact that in vs. 12 Paul speaks of this life as "at work"[2] in the Corinthians. That Paul understands the "life of Jesus" as divine power is not surprising when we realize that he is referring to the resurrection life of Jesus, for Paul frequently connects δύναμις and Jesus' resurrection[3]. Two passages, Phil. 3 10 and II Cor. 13 4, are especially important, for in both Paul speaks of sharing in Jesus' resurrection power, just as in II Cor. 4 10-11. Thus the "life of Jesus" is to be understood as the power of Jesus' resurrection life, which is God's redeeming power in the specific form in which it meets the one whose life is shaped by Jesus' death and resurrection.

It is interesting that the νέκρωσις τοῦ 'Ιησοῦ is also conceived as an active power at work in Paul's body. In vs. 11 Paul speaks of θάνατος instead of νέκρωσις, and in vs. 12a he reformulates vs. 10a in these terms: "Therefore, death is at work in us." Here it is not only clear that θάνατος is a power "at work,"[4] but also that this is the same θάνατος which is elsewhere referred to as one of the principal powers of the old aeon[5]. The powers of the old aeon were previously active within the self[6], and the power of death is still active in this way[7]. However, this passage makes clear that the continuing power of death does not simply have the negative significance of pointing to the incompleteness of the believers' redemption and of God's triumph. Although θάνατος has not yet been destroyed, it has already been conquered in that now it is forced to take the role of νέκρωσις τοῦ 'Ιησοῦ, which is not something merely negative, but stands in a purposeful relation to the manifestation of the "power" and "life" (vss. 7, 10). The power of the old dominion has been transformed into a power which serves the new dominion in its present form. Thus the fact that the believer must still await the redemption of his body and is still exposed to the powers of the old

---

[2] 'Ενεργεῖται. Cf. p. n. 4 below.

[3] Cf. Rom. 1 4; I Cor. 6 14; II Cor. 13 4; Phil. 3 10. Cf. also I Cor. 15 43.

[4] 'Ενεργεῖται is to be understood as a middle with active sense, not as a passive. This is the meaning of all other occurrences of the middle-passive of this verb in Paul. Rom. 7 5: the purpose or result construction with εἰς τό and infinitive indicates that the subject is thought of as active; II Cor. 1 6: see p. 97 below; Gal. 5 6: it would be very strange for Paul to assert that faith is *produced* through love, so the participle has active sense; I Thes. 2 13: it is likely that the "word of God" rather than "God" is the antecedent of the relative, but neither of these can be thought of as *produced* among the believers. Thus the interpretation given above conforms to Paul's usage.

[5] Cf. Rom. 5 14, 17; I Cor. 15 55-56.

[6] Of sin: Rom. 7 17, 20. Cf. 7 5.

[7] That this is a continuing aspect of Paul's life is emphasized by the addition of πάντοτε and ἀεί in vss. 10-11.

dominion does not mean that God is not yet in control of things or that the present is characterized only by a struggle between the powers of the two dominions with the victory yet to be decided. The powers of the old dominion are still active, but, in the case of death at least, God rules in that he makes use of the hostile power for his own purposes. We will see more clearly why suffering and death can have this positive significance for Paul as we proceed[8].

We found in Part I that Paul connects the motif of dying and rising with Christ with the idea of two dominions, each of which is characterized by certain powers. We also noted that in Rom. 5 12-21 the respective reigns of these powers are connected with the crucial acts of Adam and Christ, acts which can be described as the founding events of the two dominions. In Rom. 6 the founding events of the new dominion are described as Christ's death and resurrection. In II Cor. 4 10-12 Paul indicates that the powers operative in the new dominion can take on a character corresponding to these founding events. To be sure, in this passage Paul is speaking of his own existence as an apostle, but in other places he indicates that participation in Christ's death and resurrection is a continuing aspect not only of his own existence but of the existence of the ordinary believer[9]. Thus the powers to which Paul refers in II Cor. 4 10-12 are characteristic of the new dominion. In so far as the powers which determine existence in the new dominion take on the character of the events on which it is founded, existence in the new dominion also takes on a structure corresponding to these events. What we find in this passage is related to what we find in Rom. 8 13, where the Spirit has an active killing function. The power of the new dominion brings about a continuing participation in Jesus' death. We shall see that, just as in Rom. 8 13, this means that the believer's past death to the old life is maintained and affirmed[10].

Vs. 11a indicates the type of experience which Paul primarily has in mind when referring to the νέκρωσις τοῦ 'Ιησοῦ: the experience of suffering "because of Jesus." Thus the theological motif in vs. 10 is given a precise application to Paul's life and work as an apostle. For Paul the idea of participating in Jesus' death and resurrection is not a mere theological generality, but a means of understanding the particular experiences of his own life. Paul is referring to repeated experiences in which he has so far managed to survive. The fact that he, nevertheless, speaks of "death" and not merely of suffering may be a reflection of the fact that he understands his suffering as participation in Christ's death[11]. In vs. 12 Paul shifts the

---
[8] Cf. pp. 88—90.   [9] Rom. 8 17, II Cor. 1 5-7, I Thes. 1 6-7.
[10] Cf. pp. 88—90, 127—28.
[11] See also the references to death or dying in I Cor. 15 31, II Cor. 1 10, 6 9, 11 23.

formulation by referring the death to the apostles but the life to the Corinthians. This leads into vss. 13-15, where the significance of this death and life for the Corinthians is brought out. The participation of the Corinthians as well as the apostles in both death and life is emphasized in II Cor. 1 4-7. In 4 12-15 Paul speaks only of the Corinthians' share in the life. Vs. 13 makes clear what is in Paul's mind at this point. The apostles participate in death but the Corinthians in life because of the preaching of the gospel. It is because of this that the apostles suffer and it is because of this that the Corinthians share in life.

In vs. 14 Paul anticipates his discussion at 4 17 to 5 10 by referring to the future resurrection. It is significant that Paul gives so much attention to the future resurrection here. We must keep in mind that he has been speaking of actual physical suffering and of the very real possibility of death. Since Paul does not reject the body as evil, this suffering cannot be regarded as good in itself, or even as something indifferent to the welfare of the true man. Rather, it can only have positive value if God uses it to grant life. This cannot be given in advance, but depends on God's act in each new situation, and finally on his redemption at the future resurrection. Thus the new life which the Christian has been granted always carries within itself the element of expectation. Vs. 14 speaks of the future resurrection in a way which supplies an important confirmation of the interpretation of vss. 10-12 in terms of dying and rising with Christ, for it refers to being raised "with Jesus," using the familiar formulation with σύν. The phrase ἡμᾶς σὺν 'Ιησοῦ ἐγερεῖ cannot mean that "Gott uns auferwecken wird, damit wir dann mit Christus zusammen sein können," as KÜMMEL asserts[12]. Paul does not speak here of being with Jesus in the future life but of rising with Jesus. Indeed, the connection of the believers' resurrection with that of Jesus is given additional emphasis by describing God as "he who raised the Lord Jesus." The interpretation of KÜMMEL reflects the views of a faulty but influential article by ERNST LOHMEYER[13]. LOHMEYER approaches some of the passages which we are studying under the assumption that Paul is using the *formula* σὺν Χριστῷ, comparable to ἐν Χριστῷ, rather than a *motif* which can be formulated in a number of different ways. He fails to see both that all uses of σύν with Christ as object do not belong together and that the motif of dying and rising with Christ is more extensive than such use of σύν, and so commits the error of trying to interpret dying and rising with Christ on the basis of the phrase "be with Christ." It has be-

---

[12] In LIETZMANN, Korinther, I, II, 4. Aufl., p. 202.
[13] "ΣΥΝ ΧΡΙΣΤΩΙ," Festgabe für Adolf Deissmann, Tübingen 1927, pp. 218—257.

come clear to us that dying and rising with Christ is a well-developed motif which refers to the believers' participation in Christ's saving acts. "Being with Christ" or "with the Lord," a phrase which occurs in Paul's letters only at I Thes. 4 17 and Phil. 1 23, refers neither to Christ's death nor his resurrection, nor to participation in any other act of Christ, but to existence in the future life[14]. In II Cor. 4 14 σὺν Ἰησοῦ, since it occurs with the verb ἐγερεῖ, indicates the connection between Jesus' resurrection and the resurrection of the believers, and reflects the motif of dying and rising with Christ. To be sure, this phrase cannot be interpreted in a temporal sense. Christ's resurrection has already taken place while the Christian's is still future. However, anyone who sees this as a problem must recognize that the same problem is present in Paul's references to rising with Christ elsewhere. Rom. 6 5 and 8 show the same temporal disparity[15]. According to the interpretation of dying and rising with Christ in Part I, rising with Christ means basically the same thing as the ideas of Christ as "first fruits of those who have fallen asleep" and as the one man in whom all will be made alive which we find in I Cor. 15 20-22. These ideas show the same connection between Christ's resurrection and that of the believers, and the same temporal disparity. This disparity is unavoidable whenever Paul relates Jesus' resurrection to the future resurrection of the believers. The resurrection of the believers "with Jesus" is not meant to imply simultaneity. Rather, it indicates that the future resurrection will be a manifestation of the believers' participation in Christ and the saving events, which determine the new dominion throughout its extent in time[15a].

In II Cor. 2 14—6 13 Paul defends himself by setting forth his understanding of his existence as an apostle. He emphasizes the eschatological glory which is now present in the new covenant and its ministry (3 4—4 6), and the radically new situation which results from the fact that "all died" and that the new creation and day of salvation are present realities (5 14—6 2). In 4 7—5 10 we find a dif-

---

[14] The distinction between the two is pointed up by the fact that they belong to two different traditions in the early church. Dying and rising with Christ was connected with baptism in the tradition, while JACQUES DUPONT has shown that the phrase "be with Christ" in I Thes. 4 17 is part of an apocalyptic tradition which appears elsewhere in early Christianity. Cf. ΣΥΝ ΧΡΙΣΤΩΙ, Bruges 1952, pp. 39—113. EDUARD SCHWEIZER, "Die 'Mystik' des Sterbens und Auferstehens mit Christus bei Paulus," Ev. Theol. 26 (1966), pp. 239—257, attempts to trace a development from the apocalyptic to the baptismal usage. Such a development would involve a considerable change in the original meaning. SCHWEIZER's approach is similar to that of LOHMEYER.

[15] Cf. also I Thes. 4 14 and 5 10, discussed pp. 132—34. On the future verbs in Rom. 6 5 and 8 see pp. 10—12.   [15a] Cf. pp. 39—41.

ferent emphasis. To be sure, this section speaks of eschatological life, but as something which is yet to come or is present in the midst of extreme suffering. This emphasis has an important role in developing the thought, basic to Paul's whole treatment of his ministry, that his "sufficiency" is not derived from himself but from God (3 5). Paul's very weakness makes clear that it is a question of God's power and not his own (4 7). Because of this, Paul's suffering does not simply have a negative significance for him. Paul sees a positive connection between his suffering and the manifestation of the "life of Jesus," for he connects the two thoughts by means of a purpose clause (vss. 10-11). It is clear that suffering does not have this positive significance for Paul because the body is evil and the weakening of the body means the strengthening of the true, inner man, for it is precisely "in our body" (vs. 10b; vs. 11b is even stronger: "in our mortal flesh") that the life of Jesus is being manifested. The fact that the dying of the body leads to the manifestation of life in that same body is a paradox. Indeed, it is miracle, as vss. 7-9 bring out by referring to the revelation of God's power through Paul's preservation in situations in which his own impotence was clear. Paul expresses the thought that participation in suffering is purposefully related to participation in life fairly frequently. We find it in vss. 10-11, and in vs. 17, where it is stated that the present affliction "produces (κατεργάζεται)" glory. We find it in other passages which use the motif of dying and rising with Christ, namely, Rom. 8 17 (ἵνα . . .), II Cor. 1 5 and 7 (καθὼς . . . οὕτως . . .; ὡς . . . οὕτως . . .), and Phil. 3 10-11 (εἴ πως . . .). In fact, it appears that Paul relates Christian suffering to Jesus' death and resurrection when he wishes to assert this connection of suffering to new life. It can be said, then, that behind this conviction that suffering leads to life stands the pattern of the saving events. By God's power Jesus' death led to his resurrection. So also God brings life from death in the existence of the believer. But if we simply speak of a "pattern," we will not fully comprehend Paul's thought, for Paul sees a meaning to this pattern. God's redemption of man through the scandal of the cross on the basis of grace alone means the exclusion of man's "boast."[16] It is precisely in tearing man away from his boast that God redeems man, for in this boast is summed up man's rebellion against God and attempt to gain life on his own, which block the way to participation in God's gift of life. Thus God grants man life through condemning in the cross his old life of reliance on himself and his own worldly possibilities. To have one's old life condemned in this way is to die with Christ. Paul makes clear that it is for this

---

[16] Cf. Rom. 3 27 with vss. 21-26; I Cor. 1 26-31 with vss. 18-25.

same reason that his present dying with Christ leads to new life. We will see that the theme of being forced to rely on God alone, not on self, comes out strongly in the passages to be discussed in this section[17]. In the present passage this is expressed in vs. 7. Paul's continuing exposure to suffering and death, so that his existence is as fragile as an "earthen pot," has a positive significance. It serves to make clear that the power is God's and not Paul's own. Even though Paul has died with Christ to the old life of reliance on himself, there is danger that the power on which his life and ministry is based might be misunderstood as his own. In that God has claimed the power θάνατος for his own purposes and transformed it into the νέκρωσις τοῦ 'Ιησοῦ, this is prevented. In his sufferings Paul is constantly reminded of his own weakness. He is forced again and again to look away from himself to the power of God. Thus Paul's continuing participation in Christ's death through suffering maintains and affirms his past death with Christ, and so enables Paul to receive the new life which comes from God.

2. *II Corinthians 1 3-9 and 7 3*

II Cor. 1 5-7 is closely related to 4 10-12, for in this passage also Paul interprets Christian suffering by speaking of participation in the death and life of Jesus. However, different terms are used in 1 5-7, and so we must investigate the meaning of these terms in order to make this clear. In vs. 3 the theme of the section is indicated by the description of God as "God of all comfort." In vs. 4 Paul begins to relate the comfort which God grants to the affliction which the apostle suffers, and the apostle's experience of comfort in affliction to the experience of the community. Paul's thought takes on a dual structure in the next three verses because of his desire to relate the two elements of comfort and affliction to each other. In vs. 5 the θλῖψις of vs. 4 is referred to as τὰ παθήματα τοῦ Χριστοῦ and is related to the comfort by a construction with καθώς . . . οὕτως. Vs. 6 develops the relation of the apostle to the community mentioned in vs. 4. The dual structure of vs. 5 is maintained in vs. 6, even though this means that the comfort which the community receives is derived separately first from Paul's affliction and then from the comfort granted him. For the Corinthians also this is comfort in the midst of affliction, and Paul emphasizes that the sufferings which they endure are the *same* sufferings endured by the apostles.

---

[17] Cf. II Cor. 1 9, discussed pp. 96—97; II Cor. 12 7-10, p. 100; Phil. 3 3-11, pp. 115—123; and the conclusion, pp. 123—29.

In vs. 7 the dual structure of the two preceding verses is continued in the subordinate clause, where the Corinthians are referred to as κοινωνοί of the sufferings and of the comfort, the two being related by the correlative terms ὡς ... οὕτως. Vs. 7 thus exhibits in its subordinate clause the same structure and terms as vs. 5. The article in the phrase τῶν παθημάτων has an anaphoric sense[1], referring back to the previous phrase τῶν αὐτῶν παθημάτων and before that to τὰ παθήματα τοῦ Χριστοῦ. It is, then, these "sufferings of Christ" in which the Corinthians participate.

What does Paul mean by τὰ παθήματα τοῦ Χριστοῦ? Taken in isolation, the genitive only indicates that the sufferings are somehow related to Christ, and leaves open a number of possibilities for more precise definition of this relation. It might, for instance, be thought that the change to διὰ τοῦ Χριστοῦ in vs. 5b indicates that τοῦ Χριστοῦ in vs. 5a is a genitive of source, that the sufferings are sufferings which derive from Christ, perhaps in the sense that Christ has ordained them for the believers. This sense is not necessarily excluded here, but other passages indicate that it does not exhaust the meaning of this phrase. We have already seen that in II Cor. 4 10-12 Paul interprets his suffering and the help which he receives in suffering in terms of participation in the death and resurrection of Jesus. A parallel not only to the sense, but also to the terminology of II Cor. 1 5-7 is found at Phil. 3 10, where Paul speaks of participation in Christ's sufferings (κοινωνία παθημάτων αὐτοῦ)[2]. In Phil. 3 10 this phrase is accompanied by references to knowing the power of Christ's resurrection and to being conformed to Christ's death, indicating that Paul is thinking in terms of participation in the saving events. The way in which Paul speaks of Christ's sufferings in Phil. 3 10 makes clear that the phrase "the sufferings of Christ" in II Cor. 1 5 refers not only to the suffering which Paul suffers, but also to the suffering which Christ suffered. In his suffering Paul participates in the suffering and death of Christ.

When Paul uses the motif of dying and rising with Christ, the thought of participation in Christ's death brings with it a reference to participation in his resurrection life. However, in II Cor. 1 5-7 Paul relates the believer's participation in Christ's sufferings to participation in "comfort." Is there any connection between this "comfort" and Christ's resurrection? There are solid indications that παράκλησις means here the eschatological salvation which Paul often calls "life." The designation of the eschatological salvation as "comfort" is well attested in Judaism[3]. Παράκλησις is used in this sense in the New

---
[1] Cf. BLASS-DEBRUNNER, sect. 252.   [2] Cp. also Col. 1 24, Gal. 6 17.
[3] STRACK-BILLERBECK, Kommentar, vol. 2, p. 124: "'Trost Israels' ist ein zus.fassender Ausdruck, der die Erfüllung der messian. Hoffnung bezeichnet." The citations

Testament[4], and this meaning is indicated in II Cor. 1 5-7. In vs. 6a Paul refers not only to comfort but also to "salvation." This addition probably has an epexegetical function, bringing out more closely an aspect of the comfort of which Paul is speaking. This reference to σωτηρία makes clear the eschatological-soteriological significance of the comfort in which the Corinthians share. To be sure, this comfort is a present experience, but as such it is already a participation in the eschatological salvation and the guarantee of the fullness of this salvation in the future. This is brought out in vs. 7, where Paul states that the Corinthians' participation in the sufferings and so in the comfort is a ground (εἰδότες with causal sense: "since we know") for Paul's firm hope for them. Here παράκλησις takes a role which the Spirit has elsewhere. As the present experience of the eschatological salvation, it is the guarantee of its fullness in the future[5]. The connection of this eschatological salvation with the resurrection life is made clear by what follows. In vss. 8-10 Paul continues his thought by referring to a specific instance from his own recent experience of the affliction and comfort he has been talking about, but, instead of carrying through the terms θλῖψις or παθήματα and παράκλησις, he speaks in vss. 9-10 of death and resurrection. The use of the new terminology is brought on by the extremeness of this experience; Paul actually despaired of coming out of it alive. Nevertheless, the fact that Paul refers to death and to "the God who raises the dead" in connection with his experience in Asia indicates that Paul's rescue, previously included in his references to "comfort," is related in his mind to resurrection. This connection of παράκλησις with resurrection life is also indicated by I Thes. 3 7-8, another passage which refers to comfort in the midst of affliction. Paul, in speaking of the effect of news of the Thessalonians' faith, states first that "we were comforted" and then that "we live." It is clear that ζῶμεν is used in a pregnant sense. It does not refer to the life which Paul was, of course, living

---

which follow on pp. 124—26 show that the "comfort" is equivalent to the Messianic salvation itself.

[4] Luke 2 25 (cp. 2 88); Mat. 5 4; II Thes. 2 16.

[5] The view of WINDISCH, 2. Kor., p. 43, that σωτηρία is "hier ausnahmsweise nicht spezifisch eschatologisch-soteriologisch gedacht, sondern auf Rettung aus jeglicher Not zu beziehen" is untenable. Paul's sufferings do not simply lead to the rescue of the Corinthians from worldly troubles for worldly reasons. Rather, his suffering in the fulfillment of his mission leads to their eternal salvation, and only because of this do they know God's comfort also as a present experience. The particular present events by which Paul is comforted must not be divorced from eschatological salvation, for in these events Paul sees the manifestation of the same ζωὴ τοῦ Ἰησοῦ in which he will participate at the final resurrection "with Jesus" (II Cor. 4 7-14).

even before Timothy's report, but to real, full life. By Timothy's report Paul was comforted, and this meant for him a renewed participation in the eschatological life. The close connection of παράκλησις in II Cor. 1 3-7 with resurrection life is now clear. It is not directly indicated there that this present experience of the resurrection life is a participation in Jesus' resurrection. However, the phrase τὰ παθήματα τοῦ Χριστοῦ indicates that Paul was thinking of his sufferings as a participation in Jesus' death, and closely related passages, such as II Cor. 4 10-14 and Phil. 3 10-11, explicitly refer to participation in Jesus' resurrection life. Since Paul uses the term "comfort" as the second element in the dual structure of II Cor. 1 5-7, giving it a position in which it corresponds to the references to sharing in Jesus' resurrection which follow references to sharing in Jesus' death in other passages, the connection of this "comfort" with Jesus' resurrection could not have been far from Paul's mind. It was simply not convenient for Paul to express this connection while developing the thematic idea of "comfort."

This interpretation of II Cor. 1 5-7 is confirmed by II Cor. 7 3. Here we meet an unusual use of συναποθνήσκω and συζάω. Since Paul is speaking of his relation to the Corinthians, the συν- prefix in these verbs must refer to the common participation of Paul and the Corinthians in dying and life. Although there are non-Christian parallels to the idea of living and dying together[6], it would be strange in the light of Paul's usage if there were no connection here with Christ's death and resurrection. Furthermore, the word order, in which reference to death precedes reference to life, indicates that Paul is thinking of common participation in *resurrection* life rather than human companionship in the ordinary life of the world. The interpretation of these references to dying and living is connected with another problem, that raised by the word προείρηκα. As WINDISCH says, this word indicates that Paul is citing himself[7]. Since Paul expects his readers to remember that he has spoken of this previously, one would expect the reference to be to some passage of the same letter. However, scholars have had difficulty in deciding which passage this is. LIETZMANN thinks of 3 2[8]. KÜMMEL corrects him, pointing instead to 6 11[9]. If, as seems likely, 6 14—7 1 does not originally belong at this point, the reference could hardly be to 6 11, since 6 11 and 7 3 would then be part of the same passage. Moreover, both LIETZMANN and KÜMMEL relegate the most striking part of 7 3 to an afterthought which is not part of what is referred to by προ-

---

[6] Cf. WINDISCH, 2. Kor., p. 222.
[7] *Ibid.*
[8] Korinther I, II, p. 131.
[9] *Ibid.*, p. 206.

εἴρηκα. Only the reference in 7 3 to being "in our hearts" is related to what we find in 3 2 and 6 11, for neither verse has anything comparable to εἰς τὸ συναποθανεῖν καὶ συζῆν. Furthermore, both 3 2 and 6 11 are passing references to the heart in passages which are primarily developed in other terms. Thus in 6 11-13 it is the contrast between πεπλάτυνται and στενοχωρεῖσθε which is dominant, while in 3 2 it is the metaphor of the letter. Thus the dominant aspects of these passages are not found in 7 3, and the most striking part of 7 3 is not found in 3 2 or 6 11. However, the basic thought of II Cor. 1 4-7 is the common participation of the apostle and the community in suffering and comfort, and we have found evidence that this suffering and comfort in which both participate are connected in Paul's mind with the death and resurrection of Christ[10].

The connection asserted here between 7 3 and 1 4-7 comes in conflict with the theory, most recently defended by SCHMITHALS[11] and BORNKAMM[12], that 1 1—2 13 and 7 5-16 originally belonged to a different letter than 2 14—6 13 and 7 2-4. Some kind of disarrangement does seem to be present, for the account of Paul's journey, begun in 2 12-13, suddenly breaks off and is continued in 7 5ff. However, the problem is not solved by the hypothesis of SCHMITHALS and BORNKAMM. Neither of them pays sufficient attention to the strong evidence that 7 3-4 belongs together with 7 5ff. and 1 1—2 13. Not only can the προείρηκα in 7 3 only be adequately explained by connecting it to 1 4-7, but 7 4 shows clearly the connection of these verses to chapters 1—2 and 7. In 7 4 the joy which characterizes these chapters is expressed in the strongest possible fashion. SCHMITHALS, who makes a sharp distinction in the tone of the two "letters," fails to see this[13], and BORNKAMM tries to explain it away by saying that

> 7 2-4 ... den allgemeinen Grund ausspricht für die Hoffnung, die P. auf die Korinther setzt, und die Bitte, die er an sie richtet, aber noch nicht sich auf den durch Rückkehr und Bericht des Titus empfangenen Trost bezieht[14].

---

[10] WINDISCH, 2. Kor., p. 222, points to 4 12 "oder besser" 1 6b. It is possible that 4 10-15 is also related to 7 3. The common emphasis on death and life suggests this (but see also 1 8-10). However, in 4 10-15 Paul speaks only of the Corinthians' participation in life, not of their participation in death. Indeed, 4 7ff. is less concerned with the common participation of the Corinthians and the apostle in death and life than with the experience of the apostle as such. Since this *common* participation is emphasized in 7 3, the primary reference of this verse must be to 1 4-7. This does not exclude a connection with 4 10-15, for 1 4-7 and 4 10-15 are closely related in thought.

[11] WALTER SCHMITHALS, Die Gnosis in Korinth, Göttingen 1956. Cf. pp. 18—22.

[12] GÜNTHER BORNKAMM, Die Vorgeschichte des sogenannten Zweiten Korintherbriefes, Heidelberg 1961.

[13] Cf. pp. 19—20.   [14] P. 22, n. 82.

On the contrary, the strong language of vs. 4 cannot be explained as an expression of Paul's hope for the successful outcome of an issue which was still very much in doubt. Furthermore, the connection of the terms used in 7 4 with what follows in chapter 7 (and with chapters 1—2) is too close to be explained as a "Stichwort-Verbindung."[15] The connection is not a matter of one word, but of a whole series of them. Furthermore, these words are used in the same way, being applied by Paul to himself in speaking of his relationship to the Corinthians. Thus the reference to Paul's καύχησις concerning the Corinthians in 7 4 is paralleled in 7 14 and 1 14[16]. The term παράκλησις occurs nowhere in II Corinthians between its thematic use in 1 3-7 and its reoccurrence in 7 4, but from that point on it is again of central importance, occurring in 7 4, 7, and 13, while the verb παρακαλέω in the sense of "comfort" occurs in 7 6, 7, and 13[17]. Furthermore, in 1 4-6 Paul contrasts παράκλησις with θλῖψις. In 7 4 both these terms are found, and the latter is carried into vs. 5 by the participle θλιβόμενοι. The use of ὑπερπερισσεύομαι in connection with the ideas of παράκλησις and χαρά in 7 4 is paralleled by περισσεύω in 1 5 and περισσοτέρως in 7 13. Paul's χαρά with respect to the Corinthians is spoken of in 2 3 and 7 7, 9, 13, and 16, as well as 7 4. The connection of 7 4 with 7 7 and 13 is especially apparent, for we find the same combination of the ideas of comfort and joy, and, in the cases of 7 4 and 13, the same emphasis on the excessive character of this joy. These observations show that the thesis that a redactor simply inserted another letter between 2 13 and 7 5 needs to be modified at the very least. The difficulty raised by the relation of 2 12-13 to 7 5 is still present, but any attempt to explain this relation must take account of the clear connection of 7 3-4 with 1 1—2 11 and 7 5-16[18].

---

[15] *Ibid.*
[16] 5 12 refers to the Corinthians' boast in the apostles, and so makes a different point.
[17] Between 1 6 and 7 6 παρακαλέω occurs in the sense of "comfort" only at 2 7.
[18] The real problem, it seems to me, rests with 2 12-13, which shows no close connection with its context, but is obviously continued in 7 5. The difference in character which SCHMITHALS, pp. 19—20, sees between 2 14—6 13, 7 2-4 and 1 1—2 13, 7 5-16 does not seem to me so great as to necessitate two letters. BORNKAMM suggests that the reason for the redactor's insertion after 2 13 is "die Tendenz der Idealisierung des Apostelbildes" (p. 30). By connecting 2 13 with the idea of the triumphal procession in 2 14 the redactor reveals that he saw "jene Reise des Paulus von Ephesus über Troas nach Mazedonien im Lichte des Triumphzuges..., den der Völkerapostel vollbracht hat" (p. 30). It is interesting that this could just as well serve as an explanation of why a redactor (there must have been a redactor, since chapters 10—13 do not belong to the same letter as chapters 1—2 and 7) inserted 2 12-13 before 2 14, dislocating it from its proper place between 7 4 and 5. In such a case the connection of chapters 1—2 and 7 would continue to be striking, but

II B. Dying and Rising with Christ in Suffering

The connection of II Cor. 7 3 with 1 4-7 provides an explanation of προείρηκα which accounts for the whole of the rest of the sentence. Furthermore, this connection illumines both 7 3 and 1 4-7. On the one hand, 1 4-7 makes clear that the common participation of apostle and community in death and life referred to in 7 3 is not merely the result of a close human relationship, but a reflection of their common participation in the death and resurrection of Christ (cf. 1 5-7)[19]. On the other hand, 7 3 makes particularly clear that in 1 4-7 Paul was using the motif of dying and rising with Christ, for we find in 7 3 the familiar συν- verbs instead of the alternate formulation in terms of "the sufferings of Christ" and "comfort."

What we have learned about II Cor. 1 5-7 makes the interpretation of this passage easier in two respects. First, because of the reference in vs. 6 to the fact that the Corinthians endure the "same" sufferings as the apostles, it has sometimes been supposed that the Corinthians were undergoing some serious persecution comparable to what Paul had to endure[20]. This is unlikely. Paul tends to emphasize the uniqueness of his own sufferings in the Corinthian correspondence. In I Cor. 4 8-13 Paul contrasts his sufferings as an apostle with the false sense of fulfillment in the Corinthian church, and in II Cor. 11 23-29 he insists that his labors and sufferings are far greater than those of his opponents. In II Cor. 1 5-7 Paul is thinking especially of the experience described in vss. 8-10. He emphasizes there the extremeness of this experience, making it unlikely that the Corinthians were having to endure anything comparable. Why, then, are the sufferings which the Corinthians must endure described as the "same" as the sufferings of Paul? Not because they are of the same kind or intensity, but because they also are "the sufferings of Christ." The unity between Paul's sufferings and those of the Corinthians is not one of outward similarity. Rather, because they are all *Christ's* sufferings, they form one unified whole in which different individuals participate, each in his own way.

A second problem is raised by the way in which Paul relates suffering and comfort in this passage. He sees a correlation between the two, for he asserts that *just as* the sufferings abound *so* the com-

---

the προείρηκα in 7 3 would indicate the resumption of the themes of chapters 1—2 after the intervening material.

[19] I Cor. 12 26 shows a closely related thought. There συμπάσχω and συγχαίρω are applied to the interdependent members of the body. But this mutual participation in suffering and joy takes place because the members form a unity as the body of *Christ* (vs. 27). It may be that here also Christ's suffering and glorification stand behind the reference to the community's mutual participation in suffering and joy at glorification. The terminology is closely related to Rom. 8 17.

[20] So WINDISCH, 2. Kor., p. 43.

2. II Corinthians 1 8-9 and 7 3

fort abounds (vss. 5, 7) and even points to the Corinthians' sufferings as a ground for hope (vs. 7). An understanding of Paul's use of the motif of dying and rising with Christ enables us to understand this correlation. We have already encountered a similar relationship between participation in the death of Jesus and in the life of Jesus in II Cor. 4 10-11. As was indicated above[21], this positive relation not only reflects the pattern of the saving events but also is connected with the characteristically Pauline idea that through suffering the Christian is constantly reminded that his life and work are based on God's power and not his own (cf. 4 7). This same Pauline idea is expressed in another way in 1 9. Paul detects a hidden purpose behind his experience in Asia in that through this experience he was prevented from trusting in himself and forced to rely solely on "the God who raises the dead." There is danger that the Christian might fall back into the trust in self which characterized his former life. However, Paul's experience in Asia forced him to affirm the death to living to himself which had already decisively taken place (cf. II Cor. 5 14-15). Because suffering directs the believer away from himself to God and so prepares him to receive God's gift of comfort, Paul can assert the positive relation between suffering and comfort which we find in 1 5 and 7.

In 4 10-12 the death and life of Jesus are conceived as powers at work in the new aeon. This idea has its counterpart in II Cor. 1 3-7, for in 1 6 παράκλησις is conceived as an active power. This is brought out by a form of the verb which Paul uses in 4 12 in connection with these powers. The participle ἐνεργουμένης is to be understood as middle voice with active sense, as are all other occurrences of the middle-passive form of this verb in Paul (Rom. 7 5, II Cor. 4 12, Gal. 5 6, I Thes. 2 13)[22]. To give it a passive sense here would make the comfort the result of the Corinthians' endurance of sufferings. However, this comfort is clearly understood as God's gift (vss. 3-4)[23]. When the participle is understood as middle voice with active sense, the meaning is closely related to the ideas expressed in 4 7ff. There Paul speaks of the fact that, in spite of all his afflictions, he has been preserved from complete destruction. This endurance is not the result of his own power, but of the power of God or the "life of Jesus," which actively manifest themselves in Paul's body. Likewise, in 1 6 the comfort is not the result of the Corinthians' own ability to endure, but is God's power at work, manifesting itself in endurance. This verse also makes clear that God's comfort, although it may take the

---

[21] Cf. pp. 88—90.
[22] Cf. p. 85, n. 4.
[23] The references to "our comfort" and "your comfort" in vss. 5-6 mean "the comfort in which we (you) participate." Cf. vs. 7.

form of rescue from particular dangers (cf. vss. 9-10), does not necessarily mean escape from suffering, for it can manifest itself precisely in patient endurance of sufferings.

II Cor. 1 3-7 makes clear that continuing participation in Jesus' death is characteristic not only of the life of the apostle, but of Christian life in general. To be sure, the apostle occupies a special position. The sufferings which he endures in fulfilling his mission are for the sake of the church. Both the suffering which he undergoes and the comfort which he receives work to the church's benefit. But the members of the local community also share in the sufferings of Christ and in the comfort. Their lives also take on a structure corresponding to the founding events of the new dominion.

3. *II Corinthians 13 4 and 12 9*

In II Cor. 10—13 the question of Paul's apostolic authority, the dominant question in II Corinthians, takes particularly sharp form. Some of the Corinthians have serious doubts on this point and seek proof that Christ is speaking in Paul (13 3). Paul proposes to demonstrate that Christ is speaking in him on his next visit, but this will be unpleasant for the Corinthians, for it will take the form of stern disciplinary measures. In vss. 3b-4 this question of authority leads Paul to speak of power and weakness. "Weakness" was evidently a principal charge leveled against Paul by his opponents (cf. 10 10). To them only manifestations of power were characteristic of a true apostle. Paul wrestles with this charge throughout chapters 10—13. He admits in ironic fashion that in his past behavior toward the Corinthians he has been "weak" (11 21), but then takes up the idea of weakness in a positive sense. Uncomfortable at being forced to boast in his own accomplishments, he turns to boasting in his weaknesses (11 30; 12 5, 9), and in 12 9-10 he brings out the inner connection between weakness and power which has been revealed to him.

In 13 3-4 weakness and power are contrasted: Christ is not weak toward the Corinthians but powerfully active in them. This is supported by reference to the death and resurrection of Christ: in contrast to (ἀλλά) his crucifixion ἐξ ἀσθενείας, Christ's resurrection life is ἐκ δυνάμεως θεοῦ. After applying the terms weakness and power first to the community and then to the death and resurrection of Christ, Paul applies them to his own situation, and in doing so follows up his reference to the death and resurrection of Christ with the motif of dying and rising with Christ. The parallel which Paul draws between Christ's crucifixion "out of weakness" and his own weakness shows that he understands his life to involve a continuing participation in Jesus' death. Paul is not merely asserting here that his own experience is similar to that of Christ. The passages in II Corinthians which we have already studied show that Paul's thought goes deeper than that. This is also made clear by the prepositional phrases ἐν αὐτῷ[1] and σὺν αὐτῷ in 13 4, for they indicate that Paul's weakness and life from God's power are not independent of Christ but are manifestations of his participation in Christ.

The phrase εἰς ὑμᾶς applies the thought of sharing in Christ's resurrection in an unusual way. It makes clear that Paul is referring neither to the future resurrection nor to present preservation in the midst of suffering, but to the manifestation of his apostolic authority on a future visit to Corinth. Because this unusual application was not understood, the εἰς ὑμᾶς was omitted by Vaticanus and a few lesser texts, so that the rest of the clause refers to the future resurrection. But such a reference to the future resurrection would have only a vague relation to the context, while the εἰς ὑμᾶς ties vs. 4 into its context by bringing out the connection between vs. 4 and the threat of vs. 2 (cp. vs. 10). In vs. 4 Paul emphasizes the power manifest in Christ's resurrection. Christ's resurrection life is a life ἐκ δυνάμεως θεοῦ, and Christ now shows this power by his activity in the community (vs. 3b)[2]. This connection between Christ's resurrection and divine power is found elsewhere in Paul's letters[3]. However, it has a special relevance at this point. Because Paul shares in Christ's resurrection life, he also shares in the power which is manifest in that life. That is why this reference to participation in Christ's resurrection life is significant for the question of Paul's apostolic authority. When Paul comes to Corinth he will demonstrate his participation in the resurrection life of Christ ἐκ δυνάμεως θεοῦ, and this will be proof of his divine commission. Power is here closely associated with ruling authority (cp. vs. 10: ἐξουσία). In his resurrection power Christ rules over his people and his apostle shares in this rule.

There seems to be a touch of irony in vs. 4, for a demonstration of power through stern disciplinary measures (vs. 2) is not what his opponents desired. This claim to power is also balanced by reference

---

[1] This is probably the better reading, for the alternate reading is easily explained as assimilation to the σύν which follows. Here the idea of being "in Christ" is very closely related to dying and rising with Christ. On such formulations with ἐν see pp. 18—20.

[2] Vs. 3b makes clear that Paul is not thinking of an impersonal power, for the manifestation of this power means that Christ himself is actively present in Paul and the community. On the idea of Christ being "in" the believer, see pp. 59—60.

[3] Rom. 1 4, I Cor. 6 14, Phil. 3 10. See also Rom. 6 4 (δόξα instead of δύναμις), I Cor. 15 43, and pp. 84—85 above on II Cor. 4 7ff.

to the fact that "we are weak in him." This weakness is a continuing aspect of Paul's life. The weakness and the power are experienced together. These two aspects of Paul's existence seem to stand in contrast to each other, and Paul plays upon this contrast in vs. 4. However, Paul also sees an inner connection between this weakness and power. This is brought out in 12 9-10. The close relation of 12 9-10 and 13 3-4 is shown by the fact that both center around the terms ἀσθένεια and δύναμις, 13 3-4 being the first use of this contrast after 12 9-10. In 12 9 Paul reports a solemn word of the Lord granted in answer to prayer: "The power is being perfected in weakness."[4] The introduction to the account of the prayer and its answer (vs. 7) shows the reason for this connection between power and weakness. God had a purpose[5] in giving Paul a "thorn for the flesh," namely, that he "might not exalt himself." Here we have the same theme as in 4 7 and 1 9: the continuing weakness is necessary so that man might not confuse the power of God with his own power and lose God's power by attempting to rely on himself. Through 12 7-10 we see that Paul views the participation in Christ's weakness mentioned in 13 4 not only as contrasting with participation in the power of his resurrection, but also as contributing to participation in that power.

4. *I Thessalonians 1* 5-8 *and 2* 13-16

The idea of being an "imitator" of the Lord, taken in isolation from its context, could refer to something quite different than dying and rising with Christ, for dying and rising with Christ is not a matter of conscious imitation. However, when we examine the particular way in which Paul uses this idea in I Thes. 1 5-8 and 2 13-16, we will discover that what Paul is saying is very closely connected to his references to dying and rising with Christ in suffering and that these two passages have something to contribute to our understanding of Paul's thought on this point.

These two passages are parallel in thought and must be interpreted together. Both I Thes. 1 2-5 and 2 13 are epistolary thanksgivings which exhibit the typical terminology and structure of the

---

[4] Though in the best texts of vs. 9 a Paul, using the form of a maxim, speaks generally of δύναμις (the addition of μου is to be understood as a clarifying gloss), the rest of the verse makes clear that he is thinking of the δύναμις τοῦ Χριστοῦ, which is equivalent to the δύναμις θεοῦ manifested in the resurrection life of Jesus referred to in 13 3-4.

[5] Behind the passive ἐδόθη stands the action or permission of God, as is made clear by the fact that Paul prays to the Lord for the removal of the affliction.

Pauline thanksgivings[1]. The material which follows is in each case a part of the thanksgiving. Indeed, as SCHUBERT points out, I Thessalonians is unusual in that the thanksgiving itself constitutes the main body of the letter, extending from 1 2 through 3 13. In particular, SCHUBERT shows that 1 2—2 14ff. is "an indivisible entity structurally, formally and functionally."[2] Within this extended thanksgiving, 2 13ff. and 3 9ff. are repetitions which give structural unity to the whole, as SCHUBERT indicates:

> We recall that two thanksgivings of such moderate length as those of Philippians and Colossians exhibit the simple stylistic device of repeating the basic formula in order to preserve the formal unity of the thanksgiving and to complete the basic structural pattern. Indeed, we are forced to view [I Thes.] 2 13ff. and 3 9ff. as such repetitions, serving to unify formally the entire section from 1 2—3 13 . . .[3].

That the thanksgiving in 2 13ff. is indeed a repetition of 1 2ff. is clear when we compare their corresponding parts. In content the ὅτι clause in 1 5 corresponds to the ὅτι clause in 2 13. Both refer to the presence of the gospel as God's power at work among the Thessalonians. In both cases this leads to the thought of being "imitators" in suffering (1 6 and 2 14), which is then developed in the verses which follow.

The similar relation between 1 5 and 6 and 2 13 and 14 indicates that Paul sees some connection between the presence of the gospel and being imitators. Paul makes clear in 1 5 that he is thinking of the gospel not merely as words but as power. The ὅς clause in 2 13 is best understood in the same way. Grammatically the ὅς could refer either to λόγον θεοῦ as a whole or to θεοῦ alone. However, the ὅτι clause of 2 13 focuses on God's word, the key term λόγος occurring three times. Even if we were to take θεοῦ as the antecedent of ὅς, we would have to say that it is through his word that God is active among the believers. But the parallel in 1 5 indicates that it is God's word which is at work[4]. This is not surprising. The conception of the gospel as the power of God is found in thematic sentences in Rom. 1 16 and I Cor. 1 18, making clear that this is a fundamental Pauline idea.

In 2 14 Paul refers to the Thessalonians as imitators in suffering as justification (γάρ) for the statement that they really received the word of God and this word is at work in them. Being imitators in suffering, then, is understood as the manifestation of this true ac-

---

[1] Cf. PAUL SCHUBERT, Form and Function of the Pauline Thanksgivings, Berlin 1939, pp. 16—27.
[2] Quote p. 20; argument pp. 18—20.
[3] P. 18.
[4] Ἐνεργεῖται is a middle form with active sense. Cf. p. 85, n. 4.

ceptance and of the present action of the gospel upon them. The relation of 1 5 to 6 is more complex, but is basically to be understood in the same way. The καθώς clause which follows reference to the coming of the gospel in power indicates that there is some relation between the fact that the gospel was present in power and the behavior of Paul and his fellow workers in Thessalonica. This clause is a transition to the thought of being imitators of Paul which follows, for the Thessalonians were imitators of the pattern set by the apostles during their stay in Thessalonica. In 2 1-12 Paul reviews his behavior in Thessalonica in greater detail, beginning with a reference to his sufferings and trials (2 2). It is this aspect which is in mind in 1 5-6, as Paul makes clear by the participial construction in vs. 6b. The Thessalonians were imitators of the apostles in that they received the word "in great affliction with joy of the Holy Spirit." Since the apostles did not first *receive* the word in Thessalonica, the points of similarity between the apostles' behavior in Thessalonica and the behavior of the Thessalonians must be the affliction and the joy. Thus it is the *manner* of their reception of the word which shows that the Thessalonians are imitators.

SCHUBERT has called attention to the frequent use of γίνομαι, especially in the aorist passive, in 1 5—2 14[5]. It is used in places where we would expect some other verb. Especially in 1 5-7 the use of this verb is striking. The four occurrences of this verb in three verses, used first of the gospel, then of the apostles, then of the Thessalonians in relation to the apostles, then of the Thessalonians in relation to other churches, gives unity to the development of thought here and indicates that there is a connection between the fact that the gospel ἐγενήθη ... ἐν δυνάμει and the fact that the apostles were men of a certain type in Thessalonica and the Thessalonians were their imitators. Also in the content of the thought the close connection of vs. 6 to vs. 5 is clear. The reference to receiving the word in vs. 6 develops the reference to the coming of the gospel to the Thessalonians in vs. 5. Furthermore, the reference to the Holy Spirit in vs. 6 is clearly related to the presence of the gospel ἐν πνεύματι ἁγίῳ in vs. 5. The joy which comes from the Holy Spirit[6] (genitive of source) is the result of the coming of the gospel ἐν πνεύματι ἁγίῳ, and so the presence of this joy from the Holy Spirit in the midst of suffering shows that the gospel did come to them in power and in the Holy Spirit. In this particular pattern of existence can be seen the power of the gospel at work. This agrees with what

---

[5] Pauline Thanksgivings, pp. 19, 20.
[6] MARTIN DIBELIUS: "Freude ... wie sie der Heilige Geist gibt." An die Thessalonicher I, II, an die Philipper, 3. Aufl. Tübingen 1937, p. 4.

we noted in 2 13-14, where becoming imitators is also the manifestation of the gospel at work in the believers. That it is not simply the joy which is the manifestation of the gospel's power, but the joy in the midst of affliction, is made clear by 2 14 also, for it focuses on the fact of suffering in developing the idea of being imitators.

If this is the case, being μιμηταί is less a matter of conscious imitation than the result of the power of the gospel working itself out in the lives of the believers so that a certain pattern results[7]. That this is not primarily a matter of conscious imitation is also made clear by the fact that being μιμηταί is the result of suffering brought upon the believers by others, not the result of something sought by themselves. The passive nature of this is brought out by the formulation in 2 14: μιμηταί ... ὅτι ... ἐπάθετε ... ὑπό ...[8]. Likewise, in 1 6 the joy in the midst of this tribulation is not the result of human efforts at imitation, but joy which the Holy Spirit supplies or works. That the gospel works itself out in the form of joy in the midst of *suffering* is a reflection of the opposition between the word of men and the word of God. Paul makes a clear distinction between the two in 2 13. If what the Thessalonians received is the word of God, it is not the word of men. The suffering referred to in 2 14 is a manifestation of this difference and of the world's opposition to the word of God. The conflict which Paul sees here is brought out more clearly in I Cor. 1 18—2 5, where the word of the cross is described as "foolishness" to the world. There it is also made clear that the worldly status of the believers and Paul's manner of proclaiming the gospel conform to the word of the cross in its conflict with the world and its values.

The resulting pattern is shared also by the different communities in their interrelation. In 2 14 the Thessalonians are described as imitators of the Judean churches, and in 1 7 the thought moves on from the Thessalonians' place as imitators of the apostles to the fact that they in turn have become a "pattern (τύπος)" for the believers in other places. Although the idea of conscious imitation of the Thessalonians' faith is probably present here (cf. vs. 8b), it is significant that Paul explains this spread of the pattern by referring first of all to the gospel (vs. 8a). The presence of the power of the gospel among the Thessalonians has caused it to sound forth with new power to others, and with the power of the gospel the pattern is also spread.

This idea of the power of the gospel manifesting itself in the pattern of joy in the midst of suffering is related to the idea of the

---

[7] Philo offers us some examples of the use of μιμέομαι in a way which excludes a conscious imitation in any literal sense. Cf. Spec Leg IV, 83; Aet Mund 135.

[8] Ἐπάθετε by itself might have the more active sense of "endure," but the addition of ὑπό and the agent makes clear the passive sense here.

two powers of the life and death of Jesus which we found in II Cor. 4 7-12. The θλῖψις and χαρά referred to in I Thes. 1 6 correspond closely to the θλῖψις or παθήματα and παράκλησις of II Cor. 1 3-7. The connection of the basic thought to the passages we have already examined is completed by the fact that Paul traces the pattern back to the Lord. Throughout the thanksgiving (1 2—3 13) Paul is chiefly concerned with the relation between the community and himself. This explains why the reference to being "imitators" of the Lord comes in second place in 1 6 and then is dropped. The significant thing is that Paul brings in the thought that this pattern goes back to the Lord even though this is not the point which concerns him at the moment. Similarly, the lengthy extension of the thought in 2 14-16 is at least partially explained by the importance to Paul of bringing out the relation of this pattern of experience to both himself as apostle and to the Lord. After first referring to the Judean churches as supplying the pattern for the Thessalonians, Paul had to relate the experience of the Judean churches to the experience of the Lord and of himself as apostle in order to complete his thought. This he does in the course of his accusation of the Jews in vss. 15-16. The fact that the pattern which the lives of the Thessalonians take on through the power of the gospel is finally that of Christ makes clear the connection of the thought here with what Paul says elsewhere in terms of dying and rising with Christ, even though the idea of μιμητής in its frequent sense of conscious imitation is something quite different from what Paul means by dying and rising with Christ.

5. *Christ's Power of Transformation as Power of Conformation*[1]

Before we complete the investigation of the passages which refer to dying and rising with Christ in connection with suffering, it is worth while to examine a motif which, although it is distinct from that of dying and rising with Christ, interplays with it and helps to illumine Paul's understanding of the Christian's participation in Christ's death and life.

II Cor. 4 1-6 continues the discussion begun in chapter 3 by developing further the contrast between veiling and revelation of glory and applying these ideas to the problem which has arisen with regard to Paul's ministry. There is an especially close connection between 3 18 and 4 4 and 6, as is shown by the repetition of the key terms εἰκών, δόξα, and φωτισμός. In 4 4 Paul refers to Christ as εἰκών

---

[1] I will use the term "conformation" in the specific sense of the process of taking on the same form, as in συμμορφίζεσθαι, "to take on the same form."

5. Christ's Power of Transformation as Power of Conformation

τοῦ θεοῦ. The recent studies by ELTESTER[2] and JERVELL[3] have helped to make clear what this means. ELTESTER explains,

> Die Wendung τῆς δόξης τοῦ Χριστοῦ, ὅς ἐστιν εἰκὼν θεοῦ in v. 4 entspricht der Wendung τῆς δόξης τοῦ θεοῦ ἐν προσώπῳ Χριστοῦ in v. 6. Die Herrlichkeit Christi ist nichts anderes als die Herrlichkeit Gottes, die auf dem Angesichte Christi sichtbar wird; damit ist nur umschrieben, was die Prädikation "Abbild Gottes" meint: Christus als Eikon Gottes ist der die Erkenntnis Gottes Ermöglichende. Darin ist einmal ausgedrückt, daß Gott *durch seine Eikon* für den Glauben sichtbar wird, und zum anderen, daß in Christus als der Eikon *Gott selbst* sichtbar wird. Christus als Abbild Gottes ist also die Offenbarung und Repräsentation Gottes[4].

In applying this term to Christ, Paul was taking over a widespread concept, for in the surrounding world the term εἰκών was applied to a variety of mediators through whom the invisible God revealed himself to men[5]. In Hellenistic Judaism we find it applied to the figure of Wisdom[6] and, by Philo, to the Logos. It occurs with particular frequency in the works of Philo, where it is one of the chief designations of the principal intermediary between God and the world. ELTESTER summarizes this use of the term by Philo as follows:

> Die Sophia (bzw. der Logos) hat bei Philo die Funktion, Gott dem Menschen zu offenbaren; in seiner Eikon repräsentiert sich Gott für die Sichtbarkeit. Der Zusammenhang mit II Cor. 4 4 ist einsichtig[7].

In Jewish circles and circles influenced by Judaism speculation concerning such a mediator seems to have centered around the reference to God's image in Gen. 1 26-27[8]. The term εἰκών is often combined with other ideas used to connect the inaccessible God with the visible world, such as that of emanation[9].

The revelation of glory through Christ as image of God is not a matter of individual mystical experience, for it takes place through the preaching of the gospel (II Cor. 4 2-5) and affects all Christians (3 18), being characteristic of the new covenant as a whole in contrast to the limitedness both in time and in extent (Moses only) of the participation in glory under the old covenant. In 3 18 Paul indicates

---

[2] FRIEDRICH-WILHELM ELTESTER, Eikon im Neuen Testament, Berlin 1958.
[3] JACOB JERVELL, Imago Dei, Göttingen 1960.
[4] Pp. 132—33.
[5] The use of εἰκών outside the New Testament is extensively discussed by ELTESTER, pp. 1—129, and JERVELL, pp. 15—170. Cf. also EDVIN LARSSON, Christus als Vorbild, Uppsala 1962, pp. 113—187.
[6] Wisdom of Solomon 7 26.
[7] P. 135.
[8] Cf. JERVELL, pp. 46—70, 122—170.
[9] Cf. Wisdom of Solomon 7 25-26 and ELTESTER. pp. 52—54, 105—07, 150.

that the perception or reflection[10] of the glory by the believers is accompanied by a transformation. The believers are being transformed "into the same image."[11] Paul speaks of the *same* image because this image is first of all the Lord's. It is the glory-image which characterizes the Lord's heavenly existence and in which the believer can now participate. Thus τὴν αὐτὴν εἰκόνα refers back to τὴν δόξαν κυρίου, as is shown by the fact that this transformation into the same image takes place "from glory to glory."[12] Here it is not a matter of Christ being the image of God, but of the believers taking on the image of Christ. However, these two uses of εἰκών are related[13]. Christ as εἰκών participates in and manifests the glory of God to the believers (4 4, 6). It is through this manifestation of the glory of God that the Christian is able to participate in it, and this participation by the Christian means a transformation into Christ's glory-image. The transformation is a conformation to Christ's image, made possible by the fact that Christ is image of God. The idea of taking on the same image as Christ is a corollary of Christ's role as εἰκών in manifesting the glory of God to the believers[14].

This transformation is due to the Lord's power. Δόξα itself can have the connotation of power. This is the case here, for it is in seeing or reflecting the Lord's glory that the transformation takes place[15]. Also the role of the Spirit here emphasizes the Lord's power

---

[10] Κατοπτριζόμενοι is difficult to interpret with certainty, but, whether it refers to perception or reflection, it clearly involves participation in the revealed glory, as the transformation "from glory to glory" shows.

[11] On the accusative with μεταμορφούμεθα, see BLASS-DEBRUNNER, sect. 159, 4.

[12] In I Cor. 11 7 εἰκών and δόξα are again closely related. Cf. also II Cor. 4 4 and pp. 109—110 above on Rom. 8 29-30. JERVELL, pp. 174—76, explains the connection of εἰκών and δόξα here by seeing the whole discussion from 3 4 on as centering around the question of the lost image of God which returned at Sinai, according to a Jewish tradition (cf. JERVELL, pp. 113ff.), but for Paul returns in its fullness only through Christ. We do find a connection between Adam's creation in the image of God and his glory in Jewish tradition (JERVELL, pp. 100ff.).

[13] ELTESTER fails to see this relation and gives only a very short and unsatisfactory treatment of the idea of the believer taking on the image of Christ, which he distinguishes from the image of God. Cf. pp. 165—66. JERVELL is more helpful at this point.

[14] The mediating function of the εἰκών concept comes out strongly in the fact that a relation of image, image of the image, etc., can be developed into a whole chain by which each part of the world is connected to God through the mediators above it. Cf. ELTESTER, pp. 120, 123—28. Philo relates the Logos to men or an aspect of man by describing the Logos as εἰκών and men or the aspect of man as created κατ' εἰκόνα or as an impress of the image. Cf., e. g., Leg All III, 96; Plant 18—20.

[15] JERVELL, p. 175, defines δόξα as "himmlische, numinöse Machtfülle." GERHARD KITTEL shows that power is an important aspect of δόξα in the LXX. and so also

5. Christ's Power of Transformation as Power of Conformation

at work in this transformation. Whether the Lord is equated with the Spirit or not, the Spirit represents the active power of the Lord at work on the believers. The phrase καθάπερ ἀπὸ κυρίου πνεύματος indicates the source of the transformation, as ἀπό shows, and thereby indicates that this transformation is the result of the active power of the Lord as Spirit or through the Spirit.

This present participation in the glory of the Lord corresponds closely with the present participation in the "life of Jesus" of which Paul writes in the following chapter. Δόξα and ζωή both refer to the eschatological gift present in Paul's ministry, and in both cases this is understood as a participation in the existence of the risen Lord. The connection between these two ideas indicated by the development of thought seems to be this: the "treasure" referred to in 4 7 is the participation in Christ's glory emphasized in 3 18, 4 4 and 6. In 4 7ff. Paul indicates that this treasure is a manifestation of the power of God, which expresses itself in the midst of suffering as the "life of Jesus."[16] Thus there is a close connection between Paul's thought in 3 18 and 4 10-12[17]. However, we also find a characteristic difference. According to 4 10 not only the ζωὴ τοῦ Ἰησοῦ but also the νέκρωσις τοῦ Ἰησοῦ manifests itself in Paul's existence. It is the presence of these two elements that makes clear that Paul is using the motif of dying and rising with Christ. The latter element is not found at 3 18 in spite of the similar idea of taking on Christ's mode of existence. It is because Paul begins to speak of his sufferings in 4 7ff. that he brings in the motif of dying and rising with Christ. Paul has more than one way of expressing the Christian's participation in the resurrection of Christ, but the motif of dying and rising with Christ has a special role in Paul's understanding of suffering as participation in Christ.

In I Cor. 15 49 Christ is again related to the believers through the concept εἰκών. The many wear the image of the earthly man Adam or of Christ, the heavenly man. The change from an earthly to a heavenly existence to which Paul refers in I Cor. 15 49ff. is understood as a change from wearing the image of the earthly man, and so sharing in his mode of existence, to wearing the image of the heavenly man, and so sharing in his heavenly existence. The connection with the idea of taking on the glory-image of the Lord in II Cor. 3 18 is clear. II Cor. 3 18 refers to a transformation which is now in process, while I Cor. 15 49 refers to the future resurrection, the dominant prob-

---

for the New Testament. TWNT, vol. 2, p. 247, cf. p. 251. For a clear instance in Paul see Rom. 6 4. [16] Cf. pp. 84—85.

[17] That Paul connects the ideas of taking on the same form as the Lord and dying and rising with Christ will become fully clear when we compare Phil. 3 10 with 3 21. Cf. pp. 108—09. Cf. also pp. 109—111 on the relation of Rom. 8 17 to 8 29.

lem of I Cor. 15:18. Yet both are concerned with eschatological transformation, as are the passages to be considered below. The reference to the last Adam as πνεῦμα ζωοποιοῦν in I Cor. 15 45 points to the active power of the Lord behind this transformation.

In Phil. 3 20-21 we also find the idea of a transformation which is a conformation to the resurrection existence of Christ. There the relation of the new form of existence to Christ is expressed not through the concept εἰκών but by σύμμορφος. That Phil. 3 20-21 is nevertheless related to the texts already discussed is shown not only by the similarity in basic thought, but also by the occurrence of σύμμορφος and εἰκών together in Rom. 8 29. The setting in which we find the idea of conformation in Phil. 3 20-21 is important. In vs. 20 Paul asserts that "our πολίτευμα is in heaven." Πολίτευμα can have a number of meanings. It can refer to an act of government, to citizenship, to the corporate body of citizens, to the government and to the organized political community[19]. Since the ἐξ οὗ which follows must refer to πολίτευμα, it is here evidently thought of as a place, and so in the last of these meanings. It is clear here that the heavenly πολίτευμα is governed by a monarch, the κύριος Ἰησοῦς Χριστός. That the κύριος title is used to emphasize Christ's function as ruler is made clear not only by the reference to a political community which precedes, but also by the reference to Christ's subjection of the world which follows. The subjection of the world to the rule of Christ is an important eschatological motif in early Christianity. It comes out strongly in I Cor. 15 25-27, where Paul, in speaking of Christ's reign, makes use of Psalms 110 1 (LXX 109 1) and 8 7, which play an important role in this motif. The use of ὑποτάξαι in Phil. 3 21 may also be an echo of Psalm 8 7. In any case, the reference in this verse to Christ's eschatological reign is clear. The title σωτήρ applied to Christ in vs. 20 is an important royal title, and the setting indicates that it may have this sense here[20]. Even now

---

[18] To be sure, besides the future accepted in the Nestle text there is a strongly attested variant φορέσωμεν. JERVELL, pp. 261—62, presents a possible explanation for a secondary development of the subjunctive from an original indicative. Vss. 50-54 clearly refer to a future transformation.

[19] Cf. HENRY G. LIDDELL and ROBERT SCOTT, A Greek-English Lexicon, 9th Ed. Oxford 1940, p. 1434, and TWNT, vol. 6, p. 519.

[20] Cf. MARTIN DIBELIUS, Die Pastoralbriefe, 3. Aufl. Tübingen 1955, pp. 76—77. DIBELIUS does not think that this sense is present at Phil. 3 20, since there is no evidence of a contrast to another σωτήρ. Cf. Philipper, p. 93. Whether such a contrast is present or not, we do find the idea of the "Anbruch einer neuen Weltzeit" (Pastoralbriefe, p. 76), which DIBELIUS sees as an indication of the connection of this title with the "Herrscherkult," and this is related to the subjection of the world to Christ as Lord.

5. Christ's Power of Transformation as Power of Conformation

the Christian stands under the authority of this Lord, though he is not yet manifest in the world. Christ's manifestation in the world is the object of the eager expectation of the believers, for with the coming of the Lord from heaven their body will be conformed to that of the Lord. This conformation to the Lord's body of glory is a manifestation of the Lord's power over the world, for the transformation will take place "according to the power with which he is able[21] also to subject the whole world[22] to himself."[23] Along with the world Christ subjects the believers' body to his power, for it is a part of the old world. It is, then, the Lord's ruling power which brings about the conformation of the believer to his body of glory. This is a particularly strong example of the idea of Christ's power at work in conforming the Christian to himself[24].

Phil. 3 20-21 is the conclusion of a section beginning at 3 2 in which Paul warns against Jewish persecution and illustrates proper behavior in this situation by referring to himself. The final transformation of which Paul speaks in 3 21 has already been referred to in a more personal way in 3 11. The relation to Christ indicated in 3 21 by the idea of conformation is expressed in 3 10-11 by the motif of dying and rising with Christ. The close connection of vss. 10-11 with vs. 21 is shown by the fact that Paul, while thinking in terms of dying and rising with Christ, employs the unusual word συμμορφιζόμενος (vs. 10)[25]. The connection of the thought with the σύμμορφος in vs. 21 is clear. The striking thing is that in 3 10-11 συμμορφιζόμενος refers not to conformation to Christ's resurrection, but to his death.

In Rom. 8 29 we find the two key terms σύμμορφος and εἰκών combined. The conformation is a conformation to the image of God's Son. The occurrence of these two terms together and the use of each of them in a similar way in the other passages which we have exam-

---

[21] More literally: "so that he is able" — consecutive sense. Cf. BLASS-DEBRUNNER, sect. 400, 2.

[22] Cf. p. 115, n. 3.

[23] Αὐτῷ with reflexive sense. Cf. BLASS-DEBRUNNER, sect. 283.

[24] LOHMEYER, Philipper, pp. 159—162, distinguishes between the last clause of vs. 21, which refers to the eschatological subjection of the world, and the transformation, which he regards as an event preceding this subjection and a special prerogative of the martyr. This is impossible, for not only does Paul deliberately connect the last clause to the preceding clause through κατά and καί, but also he is already thinking in terms of a cosmic eschatology in vs. 20. LOHMEYER himself points out that "ἀπεκδέχεσθαι bei Pls. sich immer auf die letzte Vollendung bezieht" (p. 158), and the reference to the coming of the Lord from heaven to earth makes plain that this is not an event which concerns only martyrs as a special class.

[25] Συμμορφίζω occurs only in Christian writings and only here in the New Testament. Cf. BAUER (A—G), sub verbo. Σύμμορφος occurs only at Phil. 3 21 and Rom. 8 29 in the New Testament.

ined show that we have here a set theological motif of transformation as conformation to the risen Christ[26]. Among the chain of verbs in vss. 29-30, the connection with glory which we found in II Cor. 3 18 and Phil. 3 21 would lead us to expect this motif to be connected to ἐδόξασεν (vs. 30) rather than προώρισεν. Closer examination shows that such a connection is present in the thought. In vs. 29 Paul speaks of God's predetermination of the goal toward which the believers are being led. This goal, in its fullest form, is expressed by ἐδόξασεν[27]. But in speaking of God's predetermination Paul brings forward the thought of the specific end for which the believers are determined, thus explaining the transformation implied in ἐδόξασεν in connection with the second of the series of verbs, while the verbs which follow assert the certainty of the steps in the fulfillment of the divine plan. Thus the final goal is both glorification and conformation to the Son.

The connection of the conformation motif with glorification also helps to make clear the connection of vs. 29 with vs. 17, where we find the motif of dying and rising with Christ. Vs. 17 is a transitional verse, closing the section which precedes and stating the theme of what is to follow. The reference to glorification is further developed in the following, especially at vss. 18, 21, and 29-30. The connection of vs. 17 with vss. 29-30 does not merely consist in the fact that glorification is referred to, but also in the way in which it is referred to: as a participation in Christ's glory through formulations with συν-. The relation becomes clearer through the reference to the believers as "Christ's fellow heirs" in vs. 17[28]. The idea in vss. 14-17 of being sons and heirs, with the Spirit as witness to this, is closely paralleled in Gal. 3 26—4 7. There the thought is developed that the believers are heirs in a derivative sense, through being included in Christ and taking on his status[29]. The same thought is quickly summarized in Rom. 8 17 by the phrase συγκληρονόμοι ... Χριστοῦ. This idea is also closely related to what we find in the purpose clause in vs. 29. The designation of Christ as "first-born among many brothers" explains in other words the relation between Christ and the believers indicated by the motif of conformation. The term πρωτότοκος is a part of the theology which speaks of God's εἰκών as an

---

[26] Cf. MICHEL, Römer, *ad loc.*, who speaks of pre-Pauline tradition.

[27] The aorist here is surprising, for the context makes clear that this final fulfillment is still in the future (cf. 8 18). Since Paul is speaking of God's preordained plan, it is best explained by saying with MICHEL, *ad loc.*, that "Pls denkt hier ... letztlich von der Vollendung her: vor Gottes Augen ist die Endvollendung jetzt schon geschehen."

[28] On this phrase see further pp. 113—14.

[29] Cf. p. 20.

5. Christ's Power of Transformation as Power of Conformation

intermediary between God and the world[30]. That is why it appears here along with the concept εἰκών. However, Paul is aware of the familial relationship indicated by this term, as the accompanying references to "Son" and "brothers" show. In vs. 29 Paul is primarily concerned with the relation of the "first-born" to the "many brothers." Through being conformed to the image of Christ, the believers take on his status, becoming "brothers" of God's Son. The close connection of this with the thought in vs. 17 of being children and heirs of God as Christ's fellow heirs, which finds its fulfillment in glorification with Christ, is clear. Once again we see that the motif of dying and rising with Christ and the motif of being conformed to Christ or taking on his image are closely related in Paul's thought. At the same time it is clear in Rom. 8 17, just as in II Cor. 4 7ff., why Paul chooses to use the former motif: because he wishes to speak not only of glorification but also of suffering with Christ.

We have found through examining the passages which refer to the Lord's transforming power as conforming power that this motif occurs in proximity to the motif of dying and rising with Christ three times, and that each time there is indication of a connection between these two motifs. This is especially clear in Phil. 3 10, where Paul uses the word συμμορφιζόμενος in a passage which is structured in terms of dying and rising with Christ. Just as previously when we noted the relation between dying and rising with Christ and the idea of a corporate man or body, this connection between two motifs not only brings out the interconnectedness of Paul's thought but also helps to clarify the manner in which Paul understood dying and rising with Christ. It shows that the dying and rising with Christ which takes place in the believer's life is neither a matter of copying what Christ has done nor primarily of the individual's mystical experience, but a participation in Christ's mode of existence through his forming power. The dynamic aspect of Paul's thought is brought out by the references to the transforming power of the Lord or the Spirit in connection with the motif of conformation[31]. This agrees with what we have already discovered in the passages which refer to a present dying and rising with Christ, for there also we found reference to powers at work on the believers[32]. These powers act in a way which corresponds to the events which found the new aeon and so bring about a conformation of the exist-

---

[30] Cf. Col. 1 15, Hebrews 1 3 and 6, and Philo's application of πρωτόγονος to the Logos, as at Conf Ling 146.
[31] Cf. II Cor. 3 18; I Cor. 15 45, 49; Phil. 3 20-21.
[32] Cf. Rom. 8 13; II Cor. 1 6, 4 10-12, 13 3-4; I Thes. 1 5-6, 2 13-14. See the discussion of these passages above.

ence of the believers to these events and to the Lord with whom they are connected. To be sure, the passages in which Paul uses the motif of dying and rising with Christ go beyond what we have found in connection with the idea of conformation to the risen Christ in that they make clear that the power at work on the believer also expresses itself in dying and suffering. This is the striking aspect of Paul's use of dying and rising with Christ in connection with the present existence of the believer. The saving significance of conformation to the risen Christ is obvious, for this means sharing in his power and glory. That the Lord should require a continuing participation in his death is more surprising, but this emphasis is characteristic of Paul and is rooted deeply in his theology[33]. The power which conforms the believer to Christ can be understood as the power by which Christ rules as eschatological Lord, for, according to Phil. 3 20-21, the conformation of the believers to Christ is an aspect of Christ's conquest of the world. The full conformation of the believers to their Lord will come with the full subjection of the world to Christ. Paul knows, however, that this process of conformation is already going on in the present (Phil. 3 10), and this also must be understood as an aspect of Christ's subjection of the world. Christ's kingdom, the new dominion, is first of all established in that the Christian dies with Christ to the old lordship and enters Christ's lordship. Christ's reign expresses itself in the present in that the believers are formed by the powers of his death and resurrection. Christ's conquest will be complete when men are fully conformed to his resurrection glory. Thus Christ's kingdom takes on the form which he gives it through the events on which it is based and through the present powers corresponding to these events which are now at work within it.

This discussion of the motif of conformation to Christ helps to prepare us for consideration of Rom. 8 17 and Phil. 3 10.

6. *Romans 8* 17

Since Rom. 8 13, 17 and 29 contain related patterns of thought, we found it necessary to refer to Rom. 8 17 while considering the other two verses[1]. In this previous discussion the relation of 8 17 to its context was pointed out. Vs. 17 is the conclusion of the argument made in vss. 14-17 to support the assertion "you will live" in vs. 13. At the same time the reference to suffering and glorification in vs. 17 announces the topic which Paul discusses in vss. 18 ff.

---

[33] Cf. pp. 127—29.
[1] Cf. pp. 79—80, 110—11.

6. Romans 8 17

At the end of vs. 17 the two contrasting verbs, each with the prefix συν-, express the familiar motif of dying and rising with Christ. The fact that Paul refers here to suffering and glorification rather than to dying and rising is not strange. Paul sees a very close connection between resurrection and glorification[2], and uses the motif of dying and rising with Christ to speak of participation in Christ's "sufferings" at II Cor. 1 5 and Phil. 3 10 as well as here. Although συμπάσχομεν and συνδοξασθῶμεν are left without complement, the prefix indicates here, as in the other passages we have examined, the connection between what happens to the believer and what has happened to Christ[3]. This is shown by the preceding phrase συγκληρονόμοι δὲ Χριστοῦ. Elsewhere the genitive with συγκληρονόμος indicates what one inherits[4]. In this it follows the pattern of the genitive with κληρονόμος[5]. This is not the case here, for συγκληρονόμοι δὲ Χριστοῦ is formulated as a conscious parallel to κληρονόμοι μὲν θεοῦ (note the μὲν ... δὲ ... construction) and τέκνα θεοῦ. Τέκνα θεοῦ would indicate that these are all to be taken as genitives of possession or relationship[6]. Συγκληρονόμοι ... Χριστοῦ would, then, be best translated as "Christ's fellow heirs."[7] It is clear that the prefix expresses association with the one indicated by the genitive, for it is only with the mention of Christ that it is introduced. Because Paul uses the prefix to express association with the one indicated by the genitive, he does not refer to the believers as συγκληρονόμοι θεοῦ, as would be possible if the prefix only referred to the relation of the believers with one another. This interpretation is made certain by the parallels to Paul's thought here. The close connection of vs. 17 to the idea of Christ as "first-born among many brothers" in vs. 29 has already been noted[8]. The connection with Gal. 3 26—4 7 is even more striking. Both passages discuss sonship and inheritance. In both cases the Spirit is referred to as witness to the fact that the Christians are sons and heirs. And

---

[2] Recall the emphasis on conformation to Christ's resurrection glory in II Cor. 3 18, Phil. 3 21, and Rom. 8 29-30. See also I Cor. 15 43, Rom. 6 4.

[3] II Cor. 7 3 and I Cor. 12 26 seem at first glance to be exceptions to the rule that the prefix συν- with verbs of dying, rising, suffering, etc., indicates a connection with Christ's death and resurrection. However, see pp. 93—96.

[4] Cf. Eph. 3 6, Hebr. 11 9, I Pet. 3 7.

[5] Cf. Rom. 4 13; Hebr. 1 2, 6 17, 11 7; James 2 5.

[6] Cf. BLASS-DEBRUNNER, sect. 162.

[7] BLASS-DEBRUNNER, sect. 194, 3, point out that, while adjectives and adverbs are sometimes followed by an associative dative, "die Subst. nehmen an dieser Konstruktion mit Dat. nicht teil." So Χριστοῦ instead of Χριστῷ is not only caused by the parallel to what precedes but also reflects normal usage.

[8] Cf. pp. 110—11.

in both cases being son and heir means sharing in the status of Christ, who is the *one* seed and heir. The idea that Christians are heirs because they are included in Christ is fully developed in Gal. 3 16 and 26-29. It is in accord with this more complete development of Paul's thought that συγκληρονόμοι ... Χριστοῦ in Rom. 8 17 is to be interpreted. This phrase brings out the relation between the believers and Christ by indicating that the believers, as children of God and heirs, share in the status of Christ. This in turn indicates that the believers' relation to Christ is also referred to by συμπάσχομεν and συνδοξασθῶμεν.

In vs. 17 suffering with Christ and glorification with Christ are related by means of εἴπερ and ἵνα καί. This construction, whether εἴπερ simply refers to a condition regarded as fulfilled[9] or contains an indirect exhortation[10], presents suffering with Christ as a condition, the fulfillment of which leads to the future glorification with Christ. We have noted this sort of connection between dying with Christ and rising with Christ in other passages[11]. Paul does not explain this connection here, but from what we have found in other passages it can be said that in understanding suffering as suffering with Christ, Paul understands it as a positive participation in Christ and the powers of the new aeon. Such suffering, which in itself would be evil, is not alien to present Christian existence, but is being used by God to work his purpose of glorification. This is especially associated with the thought that through suffering the Christian is kept from trust in the flesh and forced to rely on God alone[12].

It is interesting that vs. 18, in developing the reference to suffering and glory in vs. 17, speaks generally of "the sufferings of the present age." This phrase evidently includes all the sufferings involved in creation's slavery to corruption (vss. 20-21) and in the body's unredeemed state (vs. 23). We have an indication here that Paul could apply the idea of suffering with Christ to all suffering which the Christian experiences, not just to persecution for his faith.

7. *Philippians 3* 2-11

This passage is part of an exhortation to the Philippians, who face Jewish persecution (cf. vss. 2-3). In dealing with this problem Paul holds himself up as an example (cf. vss. 3-4 and 17), and in doing so refers to his participation in Christ's death and resurrection.

---

[9] So MICHEL, Römer, *ad loc*.
[10] So Kuss, Römer, p. 607.
[11] Cf. p. 89.
[12] See further pp. 88—90.

This is a participation in Christ's "sufferings" (vs. 10)[1] and involves a process of conformation to Christ's death which continues over some length of time (vs. 10: συμμορφιζόμενος, present participle). Here again Paul uses the motif of dying and rising with Christ in connection with his own sufferings and, in so far as Paul is an example for others, the sufferings of the ordinary believer. This connection makes it proper for Phil. 3 2-11 to be considered at this point. However, this passage contains material which is important for our understanding of the total function of dying and rising with Christ in Paul's thought, and this, too, must be dealt with below.

It is essential to the proper understanding of vss. 10-11 that vss. 2-11 be understood as a unified train of thought. This is possible in spite of the seeming contrast here between "mystical" and "juridical" types of thought. After a sharp rejection of Jewish claims, Paul indicates in vs. 3 the basic point at issue by contrasting two alternatives: "boasting in Christ Jesus" and "trusting in flesh." This contrast reflects Paul's central emphasis on justification through God's grace rather than through any human accomplishments or rights. It is also basic to this passage, for it serves as a heading for what follows[2]. In vss. 4-6 Paul enumerates his advantages and accomplishments as a Jew. All these advantages, culminating in his "righteousness in law," belong in the category of "trusting in flesh" (cf. vs. 4). In vss. 7-8 Paul speaks of the radical change which took place, a change which meant giving up completely his former valuation of these prerogatives in order that he might have Christ. Vss. 7 ff. continue the basic contrast between "Christ" and "flesh" with which Paul begins in vs. 3, but the thought is radicalized. Paul has not only given up these things but everything; yes, he has suffered the loss of "the whole world (τὰ πάντα)."[3] Vs. 9 shows that righteousness

---

[1] Paul speaks of Christ's "sufferings" here and in II Cor. 1 5 (cf. Rom. 8 17) because he is relating Christ's death to his own present suffering. Elsewhere he never refers to Christ's death by speaking of Christ's sufferings.

[2] LOHMEYER (Philipper, p. 127) fails to see the significance of this contrast and its role in what follows. He translates καυχώμενοι ἐν Χριστῷ Ἰησοῦ by "in Christus Jesus preisen," connecting it to λατρεύοντες. But the translation "preisen" overlooks the role which καυχάομαι (and the related nouns) plays in connection with the emphasis referred to above. It is used by Paul both to speak of man's "boast" in his own accomplishments and prerogatives, and, in contrast to this, of the Christians' "boast," which is a boast "in the Lord." Cf. Rom. 5 2, 3, 11 in contrast to Rom. 2 17, 23; 3 27; 4 2; and I Cor. 1 31 in contrast to 1 26-29. Cf. also Gal. 6 14.

[3] LOHMEYER, Philipper, p. 134: "das All." For this sense of τὰ πάντα see Rom. 11 36; I Cor. 8 6, 15 28; Gal. 3 22; Phil. 3 21. It comes in here through Paul's desire to express himself as radically as possible. The movement from ταῦτα (these pre-

from the law is still Paul's major concern. This verse is a further variation on the contrast between "flesh" and "Christ," expressed in terms which summarize Paul's doctrine of righteousness through faith. In sharp contrast to righteousness from the law stands the righteousness from God given on the basis of faith in Christ. Righteousness from the law is also described as "*my* righteousness (ἐμὴν δικαιοσύνην)," the possessive adjective being used to emphasize this point[4]. We see, then, that the old life which Paul has counted as loss on account of Christ is described by a number of different but related terms: flesh, righteousness from law, the "whole world," and that which is "mine." It is clear that the break with these realities of the old life referred to here is the same break which we considered in Part I in connection with dying with Christ as a past event. In the Christian's past death with Christ has taken place the same break with flesh (Gal. 5 24), law (Rom. 7 4, Gal. 2 19), world (Gal. 6 14), and self (II Cor. 5 14-15). The radical change to which Paul refers in vs. 7 could easily have been expressed in terms of dying with Christ. He chooses another formulation probably because the exhortative purpose of the whole of Phil. 3 leads him to present the matter as one of conscious valuation[5]. Nevertheless, it is clear that the same decisive change is being referred to, and this is important for understanding the relation of vss. 7-9 to vss. 10-11.

The interrelation of the varying tenses in vss. 7-8 is interesting. Paul refers to his decision first of all in the perfect tense (ἥγημαι), bringing out the present significance of the past decision. This is followed in vs. 8 by two present forms (ἡγοῦμαι), with continuative force, but between them is an aorist (ἐζημιώθην)[6]. In the light of the possibility that the Philippians might submit to Jewish pressure and fall away from Christ, Paul emphasizes his repeated decision in

---

rogatives) to πάντα (all such prerogatives) to τὰ πάντα (the whole world) is indicative of this desire. For a parallel in thought see Gal. 6 14 (using κόσμος).

[4] It may be that this contrast between what is "mine" and what comes through Christ is also present in vs. 7. So DIBELIUS, Philipper, *ad loc.* However, although the two clauses in vs. 7 are of parallel construction, so that μοι and διὰ τὸν Χριστόν correspond, the contrast between gain and loss receives the main emphasis. There might well be some emphasis on μοι if the reading of Vaticanus, in which μοι comes directly after the relative and before the verb, is correct. This is the more difficult reading, for the other reading could easily arise through accommodation to the order of the second half of the verse.

[5] Cf. LOHMEYER, Philipper, p. 132.

[6] The switch to the passive here may be as significant as the switch to the aorist. Cf. PIERRE BONNARD, L'épître de saint Paul aux Philippiens, Neuchâtel 1950, p. 64, who interprets this as indicating that Paul's loss was a violence which he suffered rather than solely a matter of his own personal decision.

his present life to give up everything for Christ. At the same time, Paul cannot forget that this repeated decision is based on a past, decisive break with the old world. Past and present are held together by the perfect in vs. 7. They are held together in another way in vs. 8 by placing an aorist between the two present forms. This interweaving of past and present is important for understanding Paul's use of dying and rising with Christ. We have found reference in vss. 7-8 to the past, decisive "loss" of the world of flesh, law, and self of which Paul speaks elsewhere in terms of dying with Christ. At the same time Paul refers to a continuing process of considering all this as loss. What Paul has already counted as loss, he counts as loss again and again. The fact that Paul sometimes uses a perfect verb in the passages which refer to dying with Christ as a past event shows that even there he has the present significance of this event in mind[7]. The passages which deal with suffering bring out this present aspect clearly. These passages are to be related to dying with Christ as a past event just as past is related to present in vss. 7-8. Just as the present rejection of the old world in vss. 7-8 is the continual affirmation in concrete action of the crucial decision of the past, so the dying with Christ which takes place in suffering affirms and maintains the break with "flesh" which took place when the believers first died with Christ. The past dying with Christ and the present dying with Christ in suffering are not two unrelated things, but the same thing taking place on two different levels. Paul does not see a conflict in the fact that what has already decisively taken place must still be continually reaffirmed, for the Christian is still subject to the attacks of the powers of the old world. What has been said here on the basis of vss. 7-8 is important because the relation between vss. 7-8 and dying with Christ is something more than just an analogy. This is shown not only by the fact that both refer to the same decisive break with flesh, law, world, and self, but also by the continuation of this passage, for the conformation to Christ's death of which Paul speaks in vs. 10 refers to the same process, working itself out in suffering, of losing everything in order to gain Christ.

In this passage Paul not only refers to past and present, but also to future, for at the end of vs. 8 he begins to speak of that which stands before him as his goal, and the description of this goal culminates in a reference to the future resurrection. In considering the nature of this goal, it is important to see that just as Paul speaks of his "loss" in vss. 7-8 by slight variations on one theme, so the ref-

---

[7] A perfect is used in Rom. 6 5, Gal. 2 19, 6 14; aorist: Rom. 6 6, 8; 7 4; II Cor. 5 14; Gal. 2 19, 5 24.

erences to his "gain" are variations on one idea. Διὰ τὸν Χριστόν (vs. 7) is more fully explained in vs. 8 by διὰ τὸ ὑπερέχον τῆς γνώσεως Χριστοῦ Ἰησοῦ τοῦ κυρίου μου. These phrases are further developed by ἵνα Χριστὸν κερδήσω καὶ εὑρεθῶ ἐν αὐτῷ and again by τοῦ γνῶναι αὐτόν. Each of these phrases expresses the purpose for which Paul renounced all things, and basically they contain the same idea. It is clear that it is Christ himself who is the *Heilsgut* (ἵνα Χριστὸν κερδήσω). The idea of gaining Christ is bound in one clause with that of being "found in him," and the two phrases must be interpreted together. Since it is Christ himself who is the goal and since gaining him also means being found "in him," this clause must refer to full participation in Christ. Εὑρεθῶ ἐν αὐτῷ forms one phrase which must be interpreted as a whole. It cannot be simply explained on the basis of other references to being "found" as men of a certain type by God the judge[8], for to be found in Christ is something different than being "found faithful" (I Cor. 4 2) or being "found false witnesses" (I Cor. 15 15). Εὑρεθῶ may come close to the sense of "be"[9] or it may preserve something of a judicial flavor and so be closer to the ideas of "prove to be, be shown to be, turn out to be."[10] In any case it is the state of being "in Christ" which is the object of Paul's desire, and in this context this can only refer to participation in Christ. The unusual phrase γνῶσις Χριστοῦ Ἰησοῦ is related in meaning[11]. Διὰ τὸ ὑπερέχον τῆς γνώσεως κτλ. is a formulation of the goal for which Paul is "counting all things as loss" or "as filth" which is closely paralleled by the following ἵνα clause, which refers to participation in Christ, and by τοῦ γνῶναι αὐτόν in vs. 10, which Paul explains in terms of participation in Christ's death and resurrection. Thus the context makes clear that this is no theoretical knowledge about Christ, nor simply an existential acknowledgment of Christ as Lord, but involves participation in Christ. This seems to support DIBELIUS' assertion that "γνῶσις ist in der technischen Bedeutung der hellenistischen Mystik gebraucht: nicht vom verstandesgemäßen Erkennen, sondern vom Innewerden der Gottheit in Schau und Verwandlung des Schauenden."[12] This appears to be the most mystical of the passages which we have examined, for not only does Paul use mystical terminology here, but

---

[8] So BONNARD, Philippiens, p. 65.
[9] Cf. BAUER (A—G), *sub verbo*, sect. 1b.   [10] Cf. *ibid.*, sect. 2.
[11] LOHMEYER, Philipper, p. 133, points out that this phrase is "nicht nur bei Pls., sondern auch im ganzen NT (mit Ausnahme von II Petr. 3 18) völlig einzigartig."
[12] Philipper, p. 89. BULTMANN prefers to speak of "gnostic" influence at this point, but means thereby much the same as what DIBELIUS says above, for in "gnostic" usage γνῶσις is "ekstatische oder mystische Schau." TWNT, vol. 1, p. 693. Cf. p. 710.

he speaks in the first person singular of a burning desire, even using the unusual phrase "*my* Lord."[13] But even here we must be cautious about speaking of "mysticism." What Paul presents in the first person singular is not an unusual private experience. It is, or should be, the experience of Christians in general, for Paul is speaking of himself as an example to the Philippians (cf. vss. 3-4 and 17). Thus he is speaking of something of a different nature than his visions, which he considers to be a matter between himself and God alone (cf. II Cor. 5 13, I Cor. 14) and as containing a certain spiritual danger (cf. II Cor. 12 1-10). Furthermore, in the midst of the mystical language we find the juridical language connected with justification through faith (vs. 9). We have already seen that vs. 9 is not a foreign body in this passage, for in it Paul further develops the contrast between his own position and "trusting in flesh" through seeking "righteousness in law," a contrast with which he has been dealing since vs. 3. So the γνῶσις of Christ is not something which is separate from the righteousness which comes through faith in Christ. Finally, Paul's understanding of what it means to "know Christ" is given its most complete explanation in vs. 10. There it is clear that this is, indeed, a participation in Christ, but that Paul is thinking neither of an ecstatic experience nor of a contemplative enjoyment of Christ, but instead of participation in Christ's resurrection and death, a participation which takes place in the worldly events of Paul's life. Rather than being "snatched up to the third heaven" (II Cor. 12 3), Paul participates in Christ's resurrection and death through the experience of physical suffering. Paul here shows that he is still moving within the same type of thought which we have found in the other passages which refer to dying and rising with Christ. Mystical language is being used to describe a participation in Christ which is of another kind than that which the individual enjoys in mystical experience. In order to support this point we must now look closely at vss. 10-11.

Careful attention to the structure of these two verses is important for their interpretation. Dependent on τοῦ γνῶναι αὐτόν we have two clauses with epexegetic sense, explaining more fully what it means to "know" Christ: "... that I might know him, that is[14], the power of his resurrection and participation in his sufferings, being conformed to his death that perhaps I might attain the resurrection from the dead." That καὶ τὴν δύναμιν ... καὶ κοινωνίαν παθημάτων αὐτοῦ forms one unit is shown by the fact that in the

---

[13] LOHMEYER, Philipper, p. 134: "Nirgends hat Pls. sonst diesen Ausdruck persönlichster Nähe gewagt; immer steht, wenn überhaupt ein Pronomen hinzugefügt wird, 'unser' oder 'euer.'"

[14] Epexegetic καί. Cf. BLASS-DEBRUNNER, sect. 442, 9.

best texts both of the accusatives are governed by one article. The dependence of this unit on τοῦ γνῶναι is clear, for both δύναμιν and κοινωνίαν are accusative objects of τοῦ γνῶναι. The unit as a whole, then, is parallel to αὐτόν. Thus the thought of "knowing" Christ's resurrection and sufferings grows directly out of the thought of "knowing" Christ. That καὶ τὴν δύναμιν κτλ. is best related to αὐτόν in an epexegetic sense is shown by the fact that it is *Christ's* resurrection and sufferings in which Paul desires to participate. This cannot be separated from participating in Christ himself. Rather, it explains more closely what is involved in this participation in Christ. With συμμορφιζόμενος Paul introduces a new verbal element and so a new clause. This is followed by a conditional clause. Since the references to death and resurrection are parallel to those in the preceding unit, these clauses are best understood as also dependent on τοῦ γνῶναι αὐτόν and as providing a second epexegetic element. It is possible that εἴ πως κτλ. should be separated from συμμορφιζόμενος κτλ. and understood as modifying the whole of vs. 10, but the references to death and to resurrection are paired so regularly in the passages with which we have been dealing that it seems better to take these two clauses as one unit. Paul adds a second epexegetic element only because he wishes to bring out a second aspect of his participation in Christ's death and resurrection. The use of the unusual phrase τὴν ἐξανάστασιν τὴν ἐκ νεκρῶν in vs. 11, emphasizing that this is a resurrection *from the dead*, shows that Paul wishes to distinguish what he is saying from the preceding reference to the power of Christ's resurrection. Related to this is the change from παθήματα in the first unit to θάνατος in the second. The distinction is also made clear by the fact that, contrary to the usual order, suffering is referred to last in the first unit, so that resurrection and sufferings are bound together as equal aspects of Paul's knowledge of Christ. The kind of connection between participation in the death and participation in the resurrection which we find in the second unit (and in Rom. 8 17, II Cor. 1 5, 7, and 4 10) is here excluded. Participation in the sufferings is not the necessary means to participation in the resurrection, but an equal aspect of participation in Christ. In the first unit Paul has primarily in mind his participation in Christ's resurrection and death in his experience in the world. There participation in the power of the resurrection and participation in the sufferings are interwoven. In the second unit he refers again to present sufferings, but relates this to the future resurrection from the dead[15]. This brings with it the idea that the resurrection is the goal

---

[15] Paul refers to θάνατος rather than παθήματα because he is now concerned with the resurrection from the dead. However, the present participle συμμορφιζόμενος

to which Paul hopes his present conformation to Christ's death will lead[16]. Thus the desire expressed in vss. 10-11 comprises participation in Christ through participation in his death and resurrection both in present existence and in the future resurrection from the dead.

In other passages we have noted that Paul connects the idea of participation in Christ's death and resurrection with the thought of participation in or determination by a power or powers of a certain quality. This aspect of Paul's thought also comes out here, for sharing in Christ's resurrection means sharing in "the *power* of his resurrection." Paul's reference to conformation to Christ's death probably also carries the connotation of transforming power at work on the believer, for Paul explicitly refers to such power in other passages which use this motif of conformation[17]. In one respect Paul's use of the motif of conformation in this passage is unusual, however. He speaks here of conformation to Christ's death, while all other occurrences of this motif are concerned with conformation to Christ's resurrection glory. This unusual application of the motif seems to be a transformation of the original pattern of thought in line with Paul's unusual emphasis on continuing participation in Christ's death[18].

The connection which we find in vs. 10 between knowing Christ and knowing "the power of his resurrection and participation in his sufferings" is significant. It shows, on the one hand, that Christ is viewed in terms of the Christ event, i. e., his death and resurrection. On the other hand, it shows that the powers of Christ's death and resurrection which structure the Christian's life are not felt to be impersonal things. Through participation in Christ's death and resur-

---

shows that there is a continuative aspect to Paul's thought here. He is not thinking solely of the event of death, but of the whole process of suffering which culminates in death. Thus συμμορφιζόμενος τῷ θανάτῳ αὐτοῦ reformulates the reference to suffering which immediately precedes it in order to prepare for what follows, but it is only the reference to the future resurrection itself which carries the thought beyond what we have in the first unit.

[16] Paul uses εἴ πως instead of a purpose clause as at Rom. 8 17 in order to guard against the idea that this is something which the believer already has in his pocket. Cf. vss. 12-15. Εἰ is used to express expectation. Cf. BLASS-DEBRUNNER, sect. 375. Τοῦ γνῶναι in vs. 10 is an aorist, probably with inceptive sense: "that I might come to know." This does not refute the interpretation of the first unit in terms of Paul's experience in the world, for this passage is unique in that it presents what Paul elsewhere describes as the actual character of his present existence as instead the goal for which he is striving. He probably does this for the same reason that he emphasizes that he has not yet reached perfection in vss. 12-15, i. e., because he is engaged in exhortation (cf. vs. 17).

[17] Cf. II Cor. 3 18; I Cor. 15 45, 49; Phil. 3 21; and pp. 104—112 above.

[18] Cf. pp. 127—29.

rection Christ himself is known, for it is in this way that Christ gives himself to the believer and exercises his lordship over him[19].

Paul's thought in vss. 2-11 is complex, ranging over past, present, and future, and using several patterns of thought. At the same time, it is unified, and it is necessary to note the connection of vss. 10-11 with what precedes. Τοῦ γνῶναι αὐτόν, on which vss. 10-11 depend, simply repeats and develops the ἵνα clause at the end of vs. 8 after the intervening material, and like it is dependent on ἡγοῦμαι (vs. 8). Vss. 8-11 are one complex sentence. Why does Paul run all of these ideas together? The connection which we noted above between the break with flesh, law, world, and self referred to in vss. 3-9 and dying with Christ as a past event helps us to understand the unity of Paul's thought here. That Paul now continues to count all things as loss or as "filth" is the present aspect of this break with the old world. Following the purpose clause which begins at the end of vs. 8, this rejection of the old world is expressed through a participial construction: μὴ ἔχων ἐμὴν δικαιοσύνην τὴν ἐκ νόμου. The similar present participle within the final construction in vs. 10 has a similar function. The process of being conformed to Christ's death is part of the continuing, present aspect of the break with the old world. In it takes place the loss of all things and giving up of "my righteousness from law" of which Paul has previously been speaking, for sharing in Christ's sufferings has a role in this rejection of "trust in flesh." The other passages which we have examined have made this clear through the related ideas which they express in connection with the dying with Christ which takes place in suffering. Through this dying with Christ Paul is again and again reminded that the power is God's and not his own (II Cor. 4 7), that he must trust in God and not himself (II Cor. 1 9). That is why Christ's power is brought to perfection in weakness (II Cor. 12 7-10). Through suffering the Lord turns his servant again and again from trust in self, that is, from the whole world of "flesh." Consequently, the process of being conformed to Christ's death has a natural place in Phil. 3 2-11. Vss. 10-11 are connected to vss. 2-9 because conformation to Christ's death involves the same break with flesh, law, world, and self. Thus the dying and rising with Christ referred to in vss. 10-11 shows its connection with its context at the same time as its connection with the Christian's past death with Christ to the old world and its powers becomes clear. The thought in vs. 10 does become more complex than in the preceding verses, for the latter refer simply to the rejection of the world of flesh, while conformation to Christ's death involves a break with the world of flesh which, just because it is dying with

---

[19] Cf. pp. 99, n. 2, and 111—12.

Christ, is at the same time a positive participation in Christ. That is why Paul can speak of "participation in his sufferings" as part of his goal. Nevertheless, the importance of the break with the world of flesh which takes place through this is clear.

8. Conclusion

Through the attempt to understand Paul's use of dying and rising with Christ in terms of mysticism the way was blocked to seeing the relations of this motif with other basic aspects of Paul's theology. This contributed to the idea that there was a basic split in Paul's thought, that between the juridical and the mystical[1]. Fortunately, more recent interpretation of Paul has moved away from such a division, but, in doing so, has not adequately understood the function and significance of dying and rising with Christ in Paul's total thought. However, what we have discovered in the course of this study opens the way to seeing dying and rising with Christ as an integral and important part of Paul's theology. In particular, important connections are apparent between this motif and both the eschatological structure of Paul's thought and the basic theme of righteousness through faith.

Reference has already been made to the connection of dying and rising with Christ to Paul's eschatology, and the significance of this will be re-emphasized below[2]. However, the relation of dying and rising with Christ to the theme of righteousness through faith has not yet been adequately explained. This relation is important not only because we need to understand the interconnections between aspects of Paul's thought, but also because an understanding of this relation will contribute to our understanding of what Paul means by dying and rising with Christ. In the discussion of dying with Christ as a past event, it was emphasized that Paul thinks of the cross as an eschatological and inclusive event, involving a corporate entity. Does this mean that Paul's assertion that the believer has died with Christ is dependent on the prior supposition that Christ had some special corporate or inclusive nature which enabled the believers to die with him? Investigation of the relation between dying with Christ and faith shows that Paul's assertion is not dependent on such a prior supposition.

[1] An extreme example of this view is found in ERWIN WISSMANN, Das Verhältnis von ΠΙΣΤΙΣ und Christusfrömmigkeit bei Paulus, Göttingen 1926. On the discussion of this problem up to the time of WISSMANN's book, see his first section, pp. 1—29.
[2] Cf. pp. 127—29.

It has already been indicated that Paul does not isolate the individual but understands him as determined by his participation in the old or new dominion. Each dominion can be understood as one unit, participating as a whole in the events on which it is founded, for the life of each individual within the dominion is determined by these founding events[3]. However, we can still ask: How does it happen that the existence of the individual is determined by Christ's cross? How does dying with Christ become a reality for the individual? An answer to these questions requires a brief sketch of basic aspects of Paul's theology.

In Rom. 1 18-32 Paul indicates that the central problem of man's existence is that he has refused to glorify God, to give thanks to him, to worship and serve him, and instead worships the creature. From this fundamental sin stem the many vices which result in the breakdown of man's relations with his fellow man. This understanding of the human problem is reflected in important areas of Paul's thought, such as his use of the term "flesh." When Paul uses this term in a negative sense, he is not speaking of physical existence as such, for then he could not assert that the believers "are not in flesh" (Rom. 8 9). He is referring instead to what constitutes the norm of one's actions and point of orientation of one's existence (Rom. 8 4-7), that is, he is referring to what the physical world has become through man's worship of the creation, through his attempt to gain life for himself through the world. This attempt is based on the belief that man can gain life by his own power, for man turns to the world from God because he hopes to make the world subject to his own control. Thus man's sin can also be summed up as man's "boast" before God, and Paul can place even man's attempt to establish a claim upon God through works of the law in the category of "flesh" (Phil. 3 3ff., Gal. 3 3), for this also is a reflection of man's attempt to gain life on his own. The attempt to fulfill God's commandments becomes an expression of man's refusal to let God be God, the creator and giver of life. Man is caught in this situation. He is enslaved to sin, for every attempt of man to free himself from this sin by himself merely becomes another expression of his attempt to gain life on his own.

Man is freed from this situation by God's act of grace in the cross. It is important to Paul that God's grace in the cross not only results in forgiveness for man's past sins but actually breaks the power of sin over man. This is a major reason why the motif of dying and rising with Christ is important to Paul, for through it he can make clear that by Christ's cross the believer has been released from

---

[3] Cf. pp. 39—41.

the power of the old dominion. The cross breaks the power of sin just because it is God's act of grace. If man accepts the cross as God's act of grace, he must give up his boast, for such acceptance means the recognition that his life is based upon God's gift, not on his own achievements. Paul understands God's grace in the cross in a radical sense. It is not the grace which makes up for man's deficiencies and helps him along his way. Rather, it is the grace which meets man on his way and turns him around, for the whole direction of his life was wrong. This comes out in Paul's initial discussion of the cross in Romans, for he makes clear that God's act of grace in the cross, when accepted by faith, excludes man's boast (Rom. 3 24, 27). Similarly, in I Cor. 1 Paul makes clear that there is a reason for the scandalous form of God's act of redemption and for his choice of the weak and foolish. It is "in order that no flesh might boast before God" (vs. 29)[4]. God's act of grace judges man's boast, indeed, destroys it. This aspect of the cross comes out also in the passages which speak of dying with Christ (cf. Gal. 6 14). In fact, the destruction of man's boast in the cross means the destruction of the old self and the old world, for, as the aspects of Paul's treatment of sin, law, and flesh discussed above show, Paul sees man's existence in the old world as essentially characterized by this boast or attempt to gain life on his own. Therefore, the death of the believer to the old world of sin, law, flesh, and self of which Paul speaks when using the motif of dying with Christ points to this same destructive power of the cross with regard to the old self and the old world.

God's grace in the cross reaches its goal in faith, for in faith the destructive power of the cross manifests itself in the life of the individual. The striking thing about Paul's understanding of faith is the sharp opposition which he sees between faith and works of the law. In contrast to works, which permit man to retain his "boast" because they are a matter of "debt," faith is oriented to God's grace (Rom. 4 2-5, 16). Faith is the recognition of the grace which destroys man's boast, and so through faith this boast is excluded (Rom. 3 27). In contrast to works as an expression of man's boast, faith can be described as the surrender of man's boast. When man recognizes the

---

[4] It is interesting that in I Cor. 1 26—2 5 Paul indicates that the status of Christians in the world and the manner in which he preaches the gospel correspond to the cross, which is foolishness and weakness in the world. Here we have an example in different language of Paul's understanding of continuing Christian existence as corresponding to the nature of the eschatological event. On the connection of Paul's proclamation of the cross to his emphasis on weakness and suffering as the present form of Christian existence see ULRICH WILCKENS, Weisheit und Torheit, Tübingen 1959, pp. 214—224.

radical grace of God in Christ, he can no longer boast, for he knows that he lives from God's grace and that his boast was a lie. Since man's boast is surrendered in faith, faith also means the realization in the life of the individual of the death of the old self who was enslaved to the dominion characterized by that boast. In Phil. 3 3-11 Paul speaks of dying with Christ in connection with a clear development of the contrast between God's righteousness through faith and the old life of trust in flesh and of righteousness from law. In II Cor. 1 5-9, 4 7-10 and 12 7-9 (cf. 13 4) dying with Christ is connected with the exclusion of trust in self or exalting oneself, so as to trust in God alone. Since the death of the old self finds its fulfillment in faith, these connections are not surprising.

To be sure, this death of the old self through the surrender of one's boast in faith takes place only because of Christ's cross. Faith is not a general possibility, but man's response to God's grace. Otherwise faith would simply be a "work," a manifestation of man's attempt to earn salvation for himself, and would not be the surrender of man's boast. That is why faith, as the surrender of man's boast, is also the acceptance of the gospel, the message of God's act of grace. Because faith is dependent on God's act of grace, Paul can often speak of the death of the old self as the direct effect of the cross, without attention to the role of faith. However, since faith, as the surrender of man's boast, is the realization in the life of the individual of the death of the old self through Christ's cross, it has an important place in any complete description of how dying with Christ takes place.

The aspects of Paul's thought developed above make clear that Paul's assertion that the believer dies with Christ is not dependent on the prior supposition that Christ had some special corporate or inclusive nature which enabled the believers to die with him. Paul's assertion that the believers were put to death to the law "through the body of Christ" (Rom. 7 4) is a way of *expressing* the fact that through Christ's death the old self of the believers has been put to death, not the *presupposition* of that fact. Paul can assert that the believer dies with Christ because it is the effect of Christ's cross, as God's radical grace, to destroy the old self and the old world based on man's boast and make faith, the surrender of man's boast, possible. This means that the old life of slavery to sin is over, and a new life under a new lord has begun. Because the crucial event in the destruction of the old self is Christ's cross, Paul can say that the believer has died with Christ and can even bring in corporate patterns of thought to express this fact. In this way Paul makes clear that the continuing effect of the cross is an integral part of the meaning of that event itself.

8. Conclusion

In discussing the relation of dying with Christ to faith, we have focused attention on how the death of the old self brought about by the cross is realized in the life of the individual. This does not mean that the corporate and eschatological aspects of Paul's thought can be ignored. These aspects of Paul's thought, although they are not the logical presupposition of the assertion that the believer dies with Christ, express certain essential interests of Paul. Especially, they bring out the priority and centrality of the saving events, and reflect Paul's refusal to isolate the individual from his world[5].

The connection which we have noted between dying and rising with Christ and Paul's eschatology provides the key to understanding the relation between dying with Christ as a past event and as a continuing aspect of Christian existence. Through dying with Christ the Christian has been released from the old world and has entered the new. If this were all that Paul wished to say about God's eschatological act, he could only speak of dying with Christ as something which has already happened to the Christians. But the old world has not yet accepted God's judgment of it and claim upon it, and the Christian is still bound to this old world through his present body. This means that the Christian is still exposed to the powers of the old aeon. Therefore, the new existence which is based upon the past death with Christ takes on the form of a continuing dying with Christ. To be sure, Paul speaks of dying with Christ as a present process particularly, though not exclusively[6], in connection with suffering. However, he makes clear that the dying with Christ which takes place in suffering is also a dying to the old world, the world of "flesh" and of trust in self. It is because the decisive break with the old world must continually be maintained and affirmed that what happened to the Christian in the death of Christ also determines the present structure of his life, so that dying with Christ is not only the basis of the new dominion but remains a present reality within it and leaves its imprint upon existence there. Because Rom. 8 13, II Cor. 1 9, 4 7, 12 7-9, and Phil. 3 8-11 have made clear that the dying with Christ which is characteristic of present existence in the new world is itself a dying to the old world, they have had a special importance for this study.

There is a connection between Paul's use of dying with Christ with reference to both present and past and the frequently noted fact that Paul bases imperative on indicative. This is made particularly clear by the fact that Paul can formulate not only the indicative but also his exhortation in terms of dying with Christ[7]. How-

---
[5] Cf. pp. 39—43, 70—74.
[6] Cf. pp. 77—80.
[7] Cf. pp. 77—80.

II B. Dying and Rising with Christ in Suffering

ever, this continuing dying with Christ is not simply a demand laid on the Christian. It is also a means by which the Lord exercises his power over his kingdom. In Part II we have noted that dying and rising with Christ is frequently connected with the thought of divine power. God's power manifests itself in the midst of and by means of the weakness involved in dying with Christ[8]. It is the Lord's power of transformation which expresses itself in the believer's conformation to his Lord[9]. This is at the same time the power of Christ's eschatological rule[10]. The relation between the power and the weakness is not simply one of contrast. The weakness is the necessary means by which the power is brought to its perfection[11]. Furthermore, the weakness and dying can itself be thought of as a manifestation of God's power at work. The Spirit has a killing function[12]. The power of the gospel expresses itself in that the believers become "imitators" of Paul and the Lord in suffering[13]. Not only the ζωή τοῦ 'Ιησοῦ but also the νέκρωσις τοῦ 'Ιησοῦ is a power at work on Paul in his ministry[14]. Just as prior to dying with Christ man was subject to the powers of the old aeon, so God now rules over the new aeon through his power, which continues to manifest itself in dying and rising with Christ. Thus the believer's continuing dying with Christ to the old aeon is at the same time a positive participation in the power of the new aeon. This present dying is not only a sign of the continuing power of the old world, but also a sign of God's hidden victory over the old world. This is especially clear in II Cor. 4 7-12, where the power of Jesus' death is at the same time θάνατος, the power of the old aeon, which God has commandeered for his own purposes. In ruling over his people, God makes use of the destructive power of death, and so gives to the new dominion the structure of dying and rising with Christ.

The relation of the passages in Part II to those in Part I has been made clear through their common connection to Paul's eschatology. However, these two groups of passages play a different role within this eschatology. When Paul refers to dying with Christ as a past event, he does so in order to emphasize the *newness* of the Christian situation. The Christian has already died to the powers of the old aeon and stands within the new aeon. The passages which refer to a present dying with Christ do not annul this emphasis, but

---

[8] Cf. II Cor. 1 6, 4 7ff., 12 9 with 13 4, Phil. 3 10.
[9] Cf. II Cor. 3 18; I Cor. 15 45, 49; Phil. 3 20-21.
[10] Phil. 3 20-21.
[11] II Cor. 12 9.
[12] Rom. 8 13.
[13] I Thes. 1 5-6, 2 13-14.
[14] II Cor. 4 7-12.

8. Conclusion

they do add a qualifying comment which makes clear that this present fulfillment is of a particular kind. This fulfillment continues to be a participation in life through death. This emphasis is as characteristic of Paul as the emphasis on the radical change which has already taken place. Just as the latter emphasis comes out in Paul's argument against righteousness through law, so the former has an important place in Paul's polemic against his opponents in Corinth. In the face of the reappearance of boasting within the church at Corinth, Paul stresses the Christian's dependence on God's grace and points to his own sufferings as an apostle, which show that the eschatological reign in which his opponents think they now share is not yet present (I Cor. 4 6-13). In II Cor. 10—13 Paul answers the charge of being "weak" (10 10, 11 21) by giving this concept a positive sense and boasting in the weakness revealed in his sufferings, for it is in such weakness that Christ's power is brought to perfection (12 9). In contrast to his opponents, Paul sees a positive significance in this weakness and suffering. The fact that God continues to grant life through death protects the new life from becoming a pseudo-life which does not involve the surrender of one's boast before God, and assures that it remains God's to grant, not man's possession.

The Christian's continuing participation in Christ's death through suffering points him beyond the present to the life which God will grant in the future. Although such suffering has positive significance for the Christian so long as there is danger of falling back into his former trust in self, Paul does not understand it as good in itself. Physical suffering can only have positive value if God uses it to grant new life. In itself, suffering indicates that the body has not yet been redeemed[15], that the believer is still subject to the power of death[16] and must still await the coming resurrection[17]. This future redemption is a matter of no small importance for Paul. It is an object of intense longing[18], and is connected in his mind with the freeing of all creation from slavery to corruption[19] and with God's final victory over the "enemies."[20] We will see in Part III that in two cases Paul uses the motif of dying and rising with Christ when his primary concern is with this future redemption. It is apparent that Paul's use of dying and rising with Christ is complex, emphasizing in turn the past entry into new life, the present participation in life through death, and the future participation in the life of the resurrection. Nevertheless, a unity is visible, for this complexity is simply a reflection of the complexity of Paul's eschatology.

---

[15] Rom. 8 23.
[16] II Cor. 4 10-12.
[17] Rom. 8 17ff., II Cor. 4 14ff., Phil. 3 11.
[18] Rom. 8 23, II Cor. 5 2.
[19] Rom. 8 17ff.
[20] I Cor. 15 25-27.

Part III

Rising with Christ at His Coming

1. The Place of Rising with Christ in Paul's Thought

Rising with Christ cannot be separated from dying with Christ, for the one is the necessary reverse side of the other. Dying with Christ is meaningful only because it is related to participation in Christ's resurrection life, and rising with Christ is possible only through dying with Christ to the old world. The two aspects occur together in the passages, and so rising with Christ has already been discussed in connection with passages interpreted above. These passages need not be treated again here. Nor is there a great deal that needs to be added to what has already been said about dying and rising with Christ. Part III will simply point out the place of rising with Christ in Paul's thought and deal with two verses in I Thessalonians in which the motif of dying and rising with Christ is used with special reference to the future resurrection.

The first two parts of this study are organized on the basis of Paul's use of the first element of the motif of dying and rising with Christ. This was necessary because it is in Paul's use of dying with Christ that we find a significant division of the material. There is a clear distinction between those passages which refer to dying with Christ as a past event and those which refer to dying with Christ as a continuing aspect of the Christian's life experienced in suffering. Connected with this is a distinction in the function which the motif serves. There is no such clear distinction between references to a present participation in new life and to rising with Christ in the future. Both ideas occur within the same passage as variations on one theme[1]. Thus the structuring of this study on the basis of Paul's use of dying with Christ reflects the most important division in the material itself, and this has helped us toward an understanding of this material.

Although rising with Christ is a necessary part of the motif of dying and rising with Christ, it is not the aspect which gives this motif its importance for Paul. Paul has other ways of speaking of the believer's participation in Christ's resurrection life. We have al-

---

[1] Cf. Rom. 6 4, 11, 13 with 5, 8; II Cor. 4 10-12, 16 with 14, 17; Phil. 3 10 with 11.

1. The Place of Rising with Christ in Paul's Thought

ready considered the theme of conformation to Christ's resurrection glory[2]. Paul uses the idea of Christ as second Adam to bring out the connection between Christ's resurrection and that of the believer in his most thorough treatment of the resurrection[3]. If Paul is only concerned with this aspect, he seems to prefer one of these other formulations rather than the motif of dying and rising with Christ. It is when Paul wishes to bring out the participation of the believer in Christ's *death* that this motif has a special function in his thought. Thus we have found it used either to emphasize the Christian's past death to the old world or the continuing death which takes place in Christian action and suffering. This fact justifies the particular attention which has been paid to dying with Christ.

Nevertheless, rising with Christ is an essential part of the motif of dying and rising with Christ. Dying with Christ is meaningful for Paul because it is the means God uses to grant life. Paul often indicates that rising with Christ is the goal to which dying with Christ leads, or that dying with Christ is the necessary condition for rising with Christ[4]. Although dying with Christ is a continuing aspect of Christian life in the world, it is not a good in itself, for it takes place in physical suffering. It is only because God now grants life by means of suffering that this suffering becomes an expression of God's rule over his own. It is only because suffering leads the believers toward the still future glorification with Christ that it has a positive value[5]. The destruction of the physical body would be an evil for Paul if in the midst of this God were not redeeming the body by bringing both it and its world to their fulfillment[6]. Dying with Christ is without meaning unless God is now exercising his power for life in the midst of this dying and unless God manifests this power for life fully through the resurrection of the dead.

---

[2] Cf. pp. 104—112.

[3] I Cor. 15 20ff. A pattern of thought related to these ideas and to the idea of rising with Christ is found at Rom. 8 11 and I Cor. 6 14. There Paul indicates a parallel between Christ's resurrection and the future resurrection of the believers by referring to God as source of both. Cp. II Cor. 4 14.

[4] Cf. Rom. 8 17; II Cor. 1 5, 7; 4 10-11; 5 15; Gal. 2 19; Phil. 3 10-11. To be sure, Phil. 3 10 presents dying with Christ and rising with Christ as equal aspects of participation in Christ. Cf. pp. 119—121. This refers to Paul's present life. In speaking of the future resurrection, however, Paul switches to a cautious formulation in terms of means and end. Even in the reference to present life he speaks of the sufferings and resurrection power together, not the former alone.

[5] Cf. p. 129.

[6] On the importance of future eschatology for Paul see pp. 73—74, 78—79, 129.

2. I Thessalonians 4 14 and 5 10

I Thes. 4 14 and 5 10 are exceptions to the statement that it is particularly when Paul wishes to bring out the Christians' participation in Christ's death that he uses the motif of dying and rising with Christ. These two verses occur within the section of I Thessalonians which deals with problems of the resurrection and parousia, and so the focus of their attention is on participation in these events. In both verses there are some unusual features. Yet it is clear in both that Paul refers to the resurrection of the believers by using the motif of dying and rising with Christ. As we shall see below, 5 10 is a return to the thought of 4 14. We must, therefore, interpret the two verses together. The interpretation of each in terms of dying and rising with Christ is strengthened by the other, for features of this pattern of thought which are obscured in the one are present in the other.

The protasis of I Thes. 4 14 refers simply to the death and resurrection of Jesus without the modifiers indicating the significance of this death and resurrection for the believers which are often found in such short summaries of the saving events[1]. Paul evidently intended to indicate the significance of these events in the apodosis, as is shown by the construction εἰ . . . οὕτως καὶ . . . This construction can only be explained by the fact that Paul began the sentence with the thought that what is true of Jesus, that he died and arose, also holds for the believers on the basis of Jesus' death and resurrection. This thought would be most clearly expressed by an apodosis such as: "Thus also some have fallen asleep, but they will rise with Jesus." It is clear that the apodosis presupposes the death (κοιμηθέντας) and resurrection of the believers in question here. However, Paul leaves the connection of this death and resurrection with the death and resurrection of Jesus to be indicated by the construction εἰ . . . οὕτως καὶ . . ., and immediately moves on to the problem which has been raised by the Thessalonians: the participation of the dead Christians in Christ's parousia. Vss. 15-17 show that the Thessalonians were not so much in doubt about whether the Christian dead would arise as about when they would arise and whether they would be able to participate in the parousia of the Lord. Paul assures them with a word of the Lord that those who are still living will not "come before" those who have died, for the latter will be raised "first" in order that all together might participate in the parousia. So in vs. 14 the participation in Christ's death and resurrection, which is implied by the οὕτως καί and is

---

[1] Cp., e. g., I Thes. 5 10; Rom. 4 25, 14 9; I Cor. 15 3-4.

the presupposition for what Paul does say, is skipped over, and Paul refers immediately to participation in the parousia. In consequence, the σὺν αὐτῷ does not refer explicitly to resurrection with Christ, but to the fact that God "will lead" the dead believers "with him." Although such a formulation with σύν is frequently found when Paul speaks of dying and rising with Christ, the σὺν αὐτῷ by itself would not necessarily show that he is thinking in such terms here. It is rather the construction of the sentence in terms of εἰ ... οὕτως καὶ ..., clearly intending to bring out the connection between Jesus' death and resurrection and the death and resurrection of those who have fallen asleep, which makes this clear[2].

This interpretation of 4 14 is further supported by 5 10, where we also find Paul thinking in terms of dying and rising with Christ. The latter verse refers back to the problem with which Paul deals in 4 13-18. While in 5 6-7 καθεύδω and γρηγορέω are used to contrast those who belong to the night and those who belong to the day, i. e., the faithless and the faithful, in vs. 10 this contrast refers instead to the two classes of Christians with which 4 13-18 deals, those who die before the parousia and those who remain alive until then. In 5 10 Paul recalls and reinforces in a closing summary what he has already said in 4 13-18. More particularly, 5 10 picks up and reformulates 4 14. These two verses, the one at the beginning and the other at the end of this eschatological section, are the only references to the death and resurrection of Christ in this section, and in each case this brings with it the same thought, that of rising with Christ. The presence of this thought in 5 10 must now be demonstrated.

Attached to Jesus' name, given with rhetorical fullness, is a relative clause which refers to Jesus' death "for us." We find the same construction in Rom. 4 25, and these two verses seem to have the same function in their respective settings: to bring the section to a fitting close with a nicely constructed summary of the saving events. We would expect to find, then, some reference to Jesus' resurrection in I Thes. 5 10, just as at Rom. 4 25. This is present, but is expressed in a way which reflects Paul's special concern at this point. Ἅμα σὺν αὐτῷ ζήσωμεν does not refer to the believers' continuous life with Christ after the resurrection, for the verb is an aorist. In order to do justice to the punctiliar sense of this aorist, we must understand it as inceptive: "In order that ... we might come to life

---

[2] DUPONT, ΣΥΝ ΧΡΙΣΤΩΙ, pp. 98, 112, suggests that ἄξει σὺν αὐτῷ in 4 14 shows the influence of Zech. 14 5. He admits that this is not certain. Even if this were so, which seems to me unlikely since such σύν phrases occur so frequently when Paul refers to dying and rising with Christ, it would not affect the argument above. On the phrase "we shall be with the Lord" in 4 17 see pp. 87—88 and DUPONT, pp. 39—113.

with him."³ This refers, then, to rising with Christ, and so contains the reference to Christ's resurrection and its significance for the believers which corresponds to the description of Jesus as the one "who died for us." The σύν does not have a temporal sense, but indicates the connection which Paul sees between the resurrection of Christ and that of the believers. Participation in Christ's death is not the focus of attention here and Paul does not refer to dying with Christ. However, it is important that Paul speaks of Christ's death as well as his resurrection and structures his thought in terms of these two elements, for this is characteristic of the motif which we have been studying. This death is described as a death "for us," an idea which we found combined with dying with Christ at II Cor. 5 14. Although I Thes. 5 10 does not refer to dying with Christ, 4 14 makes clear that Paul is thinking of a connection of the experience of the believer with both the death and the resurrection of Christ. On the other hand, the way in which the idea of rising with Christ is formulated in 5 10 corresponds more closely to the formulations which we have found elsewhere. Both of these verses together show that in I Thessalonians dying and rising with Christ plays a role similar to that of the idea of Christ as second Adam in I Cor. 15, the role of the key pattern of thought through which Paul brings out the significance of Jesus' resurrection for the resurrection of the believers⁴.

---

³ Similarly BLASS-DEBRUNNER, sect. 369, 2; DUPONT, p. 183. We find the inceptive aorist ἔζησεν used of Christ's resurrection in Rom. 14 9. It is not surprising that Paul can speak of those who "watch" as well as those who "sleep" as "coming to life," for this refers to a new kind of life, the life of the resurrection.

⁴ The occurrence of dying and rising with Christ in I Thes. excludes the theory of WILLIAM E. WILSON, "The Development of Paul's Doctrine of Dying and Rising again with Christ," The Expository Times 42 (1930—31), pp. 562—65, and CHALMER E. FAW, "Death and Resurrection in Paul's Letters," The Journal of Bible and Religion 27 (1959), pp. 291—98, that dying and rising with Christ is absent from Paul's earlier letters and is an idea which Paul developed from his own brush with death in Ephesus.

Selected Bibliography

See also the standard commentaries, especially those of the Meyer series, the Handbuch zum Neuen Testament, and the Commentaire du Nouveau Testament.

Barth, Markus, Die Taufe — ein Sakrament?, Zollikon-Zürich 1951.
Beasley-Murray, G. R., Baptism in the New Testament, London 1962.
Best, Ernest, One Body in Christ, London 1955.
Bonnard, Pierre, "Mourir et vivre avec Jésus-Christ selon saint Paul," Revue d'histoire et de philosophie religieuses 36 (1956), pp. 101—112.
Bornkamm, Günther, Das Ende des Gesetzes: Paulusstudien, München 1952.
—, Die Vorgeschichte des sogenannten Zweiten Korintherbriefes, Heidelberg 1961.
Brandenburger, Egon, Adam und Christus, Neukirchen 1962.
Braumann, Georg, Vorpaulinische christliche Taufverkündigung bei Paulus, Stuttgart 1962.
Brunner, Peter, Aus der Kraft des Werkes Christi: Zur Lehre von der heiligen Taufe und vom heiligen Abendmahl, München 1950.
Bultmann, Rudolf, Exegetische Probleme des Zweiten Korintherbriefes, Uppsala 1947.
—, "History and Eschatology in the New Testament," New Testament Studies 1 (1954—55), pp. 5—16.
—, The Presence of Eternity: History and Eschatology, New York 1957.
—, Theologie des Neuen Testaments, 4. Aufl. Tübingen 1961.
Carrez, Maurice, "Souffrance et gloire dans les épîtres pauliniennes," Revue d'histoire et de philosophie religieuses 31 (1951), pp. 343—353.
Davies, W. D., Paul and Rabbinic Judaism, 2nd ed. London 1955.
Deissmann, Adolf, Paul: A Study in Social and Religious History, 2nd ed. New York
Dodd, C. H., The Epistle of Paul to the Romans, London 1932. [1957.
Dupont, Jacques, ΣΥΝ ΧΡΙΣΤΩΙ: L'union avec le Christ suivant saint Paul, Première Partie: "Avec le Christ" dans la vie future, Bruges 1952.
Eltester, Friedrich-Wilhelm, Eikon im Neuen Testament, Berlin 1958.
Faw, Chalmer E., "Death and Resurrection in Paul's Letters," The Journal of Bible and Religion 27 (1959), pp. 291—98.
Feuillet, A., "Mort du Christ et mort du chrétien d'après les épîtres pauliniennes," Revue Biblique 66 (1959), pp. 481—513.
Fraine, J. de, Adam et son lignage: Études sur la notion de "personnalité corporative" dans la Bible, Bruges 1959.
Glasson, T. Francis, "Dying and Rising with Christ," The London Quarterly and Holborn Review 186 (1961), pp. 286—291.
Grundmann, Walter, "σύν," TWNT, vol. 7, pp. 766—798.
Hahn, Wilhelm Traugott, Das Mitsterben u. Mitauferstehen mit Christus, Gütersloh 1937.
Jervell, Jacob, Imago Dei: Gen 1, 26f. im Spätjudentum, in der Gnosis und in den paulinischen Briefen, Göttingen 1960.
Kamlah, Ehrhard, "Wie beurteilt Paulus sein Leiden?," ZNW 54 (1963), pp. 217—232.
Käsemann, Ernst, Exegetische Versuche und Besinnungen, vol. 1, Göttingen 1960.
—, "Gottesgerechtigkeit bei Paulus," ZThK 58 (1961), pp. 367—378.
—, Leib und Leib Christi, Tübingen 1933.

Kuss, Otto, Der Römerbrief, Regensburg 1957, 1959.
—, "Zur Frage einer vorpaulinischen Todestaufe," Münchener theologische Zeitschrift 4 (1953), pp. 1—17.
Larsson, Edvin, Christus als Vorbild, Uppsala 1962.
Lohmeyer, Ernst, "ΣΥΝ ΧΡΙΣΤΩΙ," Festgabe für Adolf Deissmann zum 60. Geburtstag, Tübingen 1927.
Lundberg, Per, La typologie baptismale dans l'ancienne église, Uppsala 1942.
Neugebauer, Fritz, In Christus, ΕΝ ΧΡΙΣΤΩΙ, Göttingen 1960.
Nygren, Anders, Commentary on Romans, Philadelphia 1949.
Percy, Ernst, Der Leib Christi in den paul. Homologumena und Antilegomena, Lund 1942.
Preiss, Théo, "Souffrir avec Christ," "La mystique de l'imitation du Christ et de l'unité chez Ignace d'Antioche," La vie en Christ, Neuchâtel 1951, pp. 1—45.
Proudfoot, C. Merrill, "Imitation or Realistic Participation ? A Study of Paul's Concept of 'Suffering with Christ'," Interpretation 17 (1963), pp. 140—160.
Robinson, John A. T., The Body: A Study in Pauline Theology, London 1952.
—, "The One Baptism as a Category of New Testament Soteriology," Scottish Journal of Theology 6 (1953), pp. 257—274.
Schelkle, Karl Hermann, Die Passion Jesu in der Verkündigung des Neuen Testaments, Heidelberg 1949.
Schlier, Heinrich, Die Zeit der Kirche: Exegetische Aufsätze und Vorträge, Freiburg 1956.
Schnackenburg, Rudolf, Baptism in the Thought of St. Paul, New York 1964.
—, Das Heilsgeschehen bei der Taufe nach dem Apostel Paulus, München 1950.
—, "Todes- und Lebensgemeinschaft mit Christus: Neue Studien zu Röm 6, 1—11," Münchener theologische Zeitschrift 6 (1955), pp. 32—53.
Schneider, Johannes, "ὁμοίωμα," TWNT, vol. 5, pp. 191—97.
—, Die Passionsmystik des Paulus, Leipzig 1929.
—, Die Taufe im Neuen Testament, Stuttgart 1952.
Schulz, Anselm, Nachfolgen und Nachahmen, München 1962.
Schweitzer, Albert, Die Mystik des Apostels Paulus, Tübingen 1930.
Schweizer, Eduard, "Die Kirche als Leib Christi in den paulinischen Homologumena," "Die Kirche als Leib Christi in den paulinischen Antilegomena," ThLZ 86 (1961),
—, "Die 'Mystik' des Sterbens und Auferstehens mit Christus bei Paulus," Evangelische Theologie 26 (1966), pp. 239—257.
—, "σῶμα," TWNT, vol. 7, pp. 1024—1091.   [col. 161—174, 241—256.
Shedd, Russell Philip, Man in Community: A Study of St Paul's Application of Old Testament and Early Jewish Conceptions of Human Solidarity, London 1958.
Stommel, Eduard, "'Begraben mit Christus' (Röm. 6 4) und der Taufritus," Römische Quartalschrift f. christl. Altertumskunde u. Kirchengeschichte 49 (1954), pp. 1—20.
Vermes, G., "Baptism and Jewish Exegesis: New Light from Ancient Sources," New Testament Studies 4 (1957—58), pp. 308—319.
Wagner, Günter, Das religionsgeschichtliche Problem von Römer 6 1-11, Zürich 1962.
Warnach, Viktor, "Taufe und Christusgeschehen nach Römer 6," Archiv für Liturgiewissenschaft III, 2 (1954), pp. 284—366.
—, "Die Tauflehre des Römerbriefes in der neueren theologischen Diskussion," Archiv für Liturgiewissenschaft V, 2 (1958), pp. 274—332.
Wikenhauser, Alfred, Pauline Mysticism, New York 1960.
Wilson, William E., "The Development of Paul's Doctrine of Dying and Rising again with Christ," The Expository Times 42 (1930—31), pp. 562—65.

www.ingramcontent.com/pod-product-compliance
Lightning Source LLC
Chambersburg PA
CBHW072153160426
43197CB00012B/2364